SPECIAL PRAISE FOR
Not Always Happy

"*Not Always Happy* is the book that, as a parent of a child with Down syndrome, I have always wanted to read. And, it is the book that I want everyone else to read. . . . drawn with humor and without the opportunistic sentimentality so often used in the literary treatment of disability."

—**CATIA MALAQUIAS**, *founder and director of Starting With Julius,*
director of Down Syndrome Australia and the Attitude Foundation

"Intimate, entertaining, at times hilarious . . . it illustrates that parenting a child with disabilities is really no different than parenting any other child. What is different are the attitudes and obstacles encountered along the way—and that's the problem we, as a community, still need to solve!"

—**PETER V. BERNS**, *Chief Executive Officer, The Arc*

". . . I found myself nodding, laughing, and grumbling audibly—each story feeling frustratingly familiar to me, bringing back memories of my experiences as a disabled person who received a public education. . . . *Not Always Happy* [is] a gem that's worth the read."

—**EMILY LADAU**, *wordsiwheelby.com, Editor in Chief of the*
Rooted in Rights Blog, Host of The Accessible Stall

"With wit, insight, and humor, Wagner-Peck has a written a book for all parents because it gives us the true power of unconditional love."

—BOB KEYES, *Arts Reporter at the Portland Press Herald/
Maine Sunday Telegram*

"I don't have much in common with Kari's experience yet I remained glued to her story, gulping it down in two sessions. Your own parenting trajectory need not be the same as hers to understand, sympathize, and thoroughly enjoy hers."

—MERIAH NICHOLS, *meriahnichols.com*

"Her easy conversational writing will keep you turning pages to see what happens next. . . . books about Down syndrome either have made me want to kill myself with their list of all the terrible things about having a baby with Down syndrome or puke at the blessings of it all. *Not Always Happy* was something that I could relate to and laugh with, and it helped me see Thorin for who he is, not the extra chromosome he has."

—LIN RUBRIGHT, *mother of six, advocate and founder of
Anna Foundation for Inclusive Education*

"*Not Always Happy* is a book you'll be glad to read thanks to Kari Wagner-Peck's wry humor, unvarnished observations, and memorable anecdotes about her son. . . . Parents of children with disabilities will relate to this mother's metamorphosis into an advocate."

—ELLEN SEIDMAN, *lovethatmax.com*

Not Always Happy

Not Always Happy

An Unusual Parenting Journey

KARI WAGNER-PECK

CENTRAL RECOVERY PRESS

Las Vegas

Central Recovery Press (CRP) is committed to publishing exceptional materials addressing addiction treatment, recovery, and behavioral healthcare topics.

For more information, visit www.centralrecoverypress.com.

Publisher: Central Recovery Press
         3321 N. Buffalo Drive
         Las Vegas, NV 89129

22 21 20 19 18 17   1 2 3 4 5

Library of Congress Cataloging-in-Publication Data

Names: Wagner-Peck, Kari, author.
Title: Not always happy : an unusual parenting journey / Kari Wagner-Peck.
Description: Las Vegas : Central Recovery Press, 2017.
Identifiers: LCCN 2016059564 (print) | LCCN 2017001779 (ebook) | ISBN 9781942094371 (paperback) | ISBN 9781942094388 (e-book)
Subjects: LCSH: Adopted children—United States. | Children with disabilities—Education—United States. | Home schooling—United States. | Parenting—United States. | BISAC: BIOGRAPHY & AUTOBIOGRAPHY / Personal Memoirs. | FAMILY & RELATIONSHIPS / Children with Special Needs. | FAMILY & RELATIONSHIPS / Adoption & Fostering.
Classification: LCC HV875.55 .W34 2017 (print) | LCC HV875.55 (ebook) | DDC 362.3/3092 [B] —dc23
LC record available at https://lccn.loc.gov/2016059564

Photo of Kari Wagner-Peck by Betsy Carson, All Art Media

Cover and interior design and layout by Marisa Jackson.

FOR WARD,
THORIN,
AND JADE

Table of Contents

Foreword

Stories of happy families triumphing over disabilities, intellectual or otherwise, tend to be false. If somebody gave you this book hoping to give you a smile and a tear and a lump in your throat and a tugging sensation in your heart, call them and tell them they shouldn't have.

If *you* bought this book expecting that kind of cheap uplift, go back to the bookstore and look for something with dogs.

But keep this book anyway. Keep it and read it so you can find out what really happens in a family where one member has Down syndrome. See what they see, learn what they learn, get a handle on a dimension of human existence that journalists and commentators and educators and other experts so often fail to understand. One that they fail to understand because they fail to see, because they refuse to see.

I don't really know Kari Wagner-Peck. We have never met in person, and I'm not sure I could pick her out of a lineup; we are not Facebook friends or book-club buddies, though I do keep tabs on her Twitter tweets.

I follow her because she is a writer who is on to something. She and her husband and their young son are participants in—or better, leaders of—a movement that promises profound changes in our world's understanding of people with intellectual disabilities. They are grappling with something that has long perplexed me—how to get people to stop misunderstanding and mistreating those with intellectual differences. Not by scolding and shaming them into pity and forced tolerance—though some of the people in this book could use scolding and shaming—but by getting them to see what should be so obvious: our shared humanity.

Kari and her husband, Ward, adopted their little boy, Thorin, from a social-service agency in Maine. Why and how they did this, and what and who stood in their way, are for you to discover in these pages. But you may—spoiler alert—not come away fully understanding what motivated this couple to create this family. They might have been inspired by a traditional religious sensibility, but Kari says she doesn't have that. Or, by a heroic hunger for parental greatness. I think Kari would say she's pretty sure she doesn't have that, either.

I'm not sure that even Kari can explain it, other than she and her husband love their boy, as intensely and irrevocably as if he had been born to them. And apart from all this love, which they seem to have in truckloads, there is something else they don't have.

What they lack is the belief, seemingly universal in middle-class, status-conscious, primed-for-perfection America, that a child born with an intellectual difference—Down syndrome, autism, Fragile X, whatever—represents an unspeakable tragedy. A fate that promises only struggle, heartache, and pain.

I don't mean to play down the challenges of bringing a child into a world full of cruelty and ignorance. Or, the dread parents may feel if they believe they are not up to raising, or loving, a child with unexpected needs. But Kari and Ward somehow reacted differently when Thorin came into their lives.

When they learned that their possible future son had Down syndrome, they . . . shrugged, basically, and got on with the adoption. It was a profoundly countercultural reaction. Somehow they never doubted that Thorin is as human as they are, no matter how many chromosomes his cells contain.

I don't want to get carried away with the awesomeness of Kari and Ward. This could be a great parenting guide, if you could read it and tease out what to do and what not to do when rearing a child with Down syndrome, but Kari—hah!—does not sort any of that out for you. This book, like life, has no user's guide.

What follows instead is a chronicle of honesty, of mistakes, of love and messiness, of laughter, of pee. It's a journey of panic and course corrections and sweet, surprising successes. Kari has troubles with homeschooling: "I forgot a lot of people wanted to be home with their children all day. I had never been that person." Kari is awful with bureaucrats. Some of them are awful to her. Kari cries a lot. She feels, deeply.

And it's also a story of a boy. Thorin is slow, but he is smart. He has trouble speaking, but he communicates brilliantly. He is adorable, but he is a pain in the ass. He is, in other words, a human child, no less and no more than your special darling with the bumper sticker for student of the month.

That portrait of Thorin is what makes this a deeply subversive book. And, an important one. If you want to be inspired by heroism amid tragedy, go feel sorry for some other family.

Heroism? Tragedy? Screw that. Kari doesn't want your sympathy. Neither does Thorin. They just want you to read this book.

—Lawrence Downes

Acknowledgments

I want to thank my husband, Ward, whose love made everything else possible, and Thorin who continues to give us the best adventure of our lives and gave me permission to write about him. To my mom, Mary Myhers Wagner, who died before seeing the publication of this book, for being a great Bubba, a generous support, and the biggest fan of my writing; to the memory of my dad, Monk Wagner, who was removed from his mother at three years old and raised by a family who loved him dearly and would have adored Thorin. To my sister, Betty Wagner, who is my touchstone, and my brother-in-law Matt Anson for their generous support of our family. To Jade Beaudoin for allowing me to tell part of her story. To Liz Peck (aka Grammy) for her generous support, and to Stan and Nancy Peck (aka Pop-Pop and Nana) for their generous support.

To Kelly Fernald, my dear and loving friend, for giving me a place to write, and to she and her wife, Allison Reid, for supporting our mission with their incredible generosity, and to Trish Waldron for being at the ready. Deep and abiding gratitude to my agent, Edite Kroll, who believes in me and is my copartner in this endeavor becoming a reality. To the memory of Elisabeth Wilkins Lombardo for being a good editor and mentor; to Lawrence Downes for championing me; and to David Kutcha for helping me shape my story. To Bess Welden, who amplifies my words and mission. Thanks to Bob Keyes for his longstanding support of my work and mission. For giving my words a home, I thank Ellen Seidman, Meriah Nichols, Louise Kinross, and KJ Dell'Antonia. To Central Recovery Press for believing in my story and for giving *Not Always Happy* the right home. Gratitude to my editor Janet Ottenweller for her skill and patience, to Valerie Killeen, Patrick Hughes, Eliza Tutellier, and the entire CRP team. Profound thanks and gratitude to everyone who reads my blog. You get me. And, thanks to the Maine Art Commission for its generous support of my work; it has made such a difference.

CHAPTER ONE

Hitting the Kid Jackpot

When my husband and I started dating in 2002, I was forty-two years old and Ward was twenty-nine. Four years later, we married and decided we wanted a child. There was a brief exploration into fertility counseling, but I realized for this to work one of us would have to become pregnant and I didn't want it to be me. I cancelled our introductory appointment at the clinic—twice—before I got up the nerve to tell Ward the truth. Understandably it took him some months to come to terms with the fact that adoption would be our path to a child.

Two years later, we stood next to each other in our dining room listening to a voicemail that had been left by Linda, a foster care worker in Maine's Department of Health and Human Services (DHHS).

"Hi guys! I met someone today who might be a match for you. He's been in a foster home for the last year. He's a beautiful boy who's two years old and . . . he has Down syndrome. Let me know what you think!"

She wondered what we thought? We felt we had made it quite clear the biggest disability we were capable of coping with was a child who was left-handed or color-blind.

I asked Ward, "Did she say Down syndrome?"

"We better listen to that message again."

We listened to the message six times until we were absolutely convinced she said Down syndrome.

"I don't know why, but that doesn't bother me," said Ward.

"Me either. Why is that?"

"For some reason, it's like I'm relieved. Everyone has something. We just know what his something is."

He was right. We had learned that everyone in foster care—and in life—has something that makes him or her more vulnerable. I looked up at my husband. His gaze seemed to follow some unseen course into the future. Neither of us said anything for a couple of minutes.

"Do you feel calm?" I asked as I broke our shared silence. "Because I feel calm."

"I do."

The next day, I called Linda and told her we were interested.

"Great. I won't know anything for a while but I can tell you his name is Thorin."

"Oh, I love that name!"

"Have you heard it before?" She sounded surprised.

"Never," I giggled. Then I asked, "What's he like?"

"What's he like? He's two."

"You can't give me anything?" I pleaded.

"Okay, he's beautiful, seems like a funny kid. He can't walk yet or talk much but he's trying very hard to do both."

While I was thinking what to ask next, Linda added, "Don't worry about this, but Thorin hasn't had his parental rights terminated. Right now, he's technically in reunification with his family."

We said we wouldn't do that—take a child who wasn't legally free for adoption—but we'd also said we didn't want a child with a disability. I started to wonder—were we being bamboozled or was it magical like the Yellow Brick Road?

"Okay." I could hear the tentativeness in my voice.

"Don't worry. The court date for the termination hearing is in two months. He won't be placed with you until that happens."

———

I started researching online. "Down syndrome and adoption" brought up mostly Christian websites. Some people who choose to adopt an infant or child with Down syndrome are religiously motivated—that wasn't us. We were only interested in Thorin who had Down syndrome.

During my research, I was shocked by a statistic I found: 60 to 90 percent of women who discover they are pregnant will abort a fetus that tests positive for Down syndrome. I had no moral judgment of their decision. I did, however, find it interesting we were considering an option most people would reject given the choice.

Wanting to learn more than what Google provided, I called friends I knew who had connections to parents of a child with Down syndrome. Without exception, the first thing anyone talked about was "grief." The stories were essentially the same: parents not getting the child they had planned on, the one without Down syndrome. A woman who had a teenage son with Down syndrome was shocked we would consider this type of adoption.

"I love our son," she said, "but I wouldn't seek it out." She wondered if we, too, would end up grieving about who he could have been.

I knew of Thorin for only a few weeks, but her comment made me angry. I wanted to say, "How about focusing on who he *is*?"

When we shared our news with friends and family, I hoped to receive some excitement. Instead, we found out what people really think about kids with Down syndrome. No one said anything close to "Hey awesome, you found a kid!" It was more like "Why do you want to do that to yourself?"; "That sounds hard"; or even "Don't do that, please."

Every day, I discovered some new tidbit of information from the Internet or a parent about what to expect when you're expecting your "Down syndrome child." It all got to me. I started to panic. We were agreeing to Thorin because of a feeling—which now seemed puny against all this information—and I actually started questioning our decision. But instead of telling Ward that, I baited him with all the horrible details, hoping he too might come to his senses. The last straw for Ward was when I told him that I had talked to a woman who said she and her husband needed to change their son's diapers when he was thirteen years old.

"So, do you think you could change a thirteen-year-old's diaper? I mean, really, could you?"

"If it was just any thirteen-year-old boy, no," he said, "but if it was our son, I could."

That was the heart of it: Thorin was not just any boy.

"Hearing all of this is frightening," I told Ward.

"So stop listening to it, Kid."

And, that is exactly what I did. I also understood why a woman might feel like she should have an abortion. The information I read was one-sided and biased. And as we would later discover, it was not an accurate reflection of people who live with Down syndrome.

When we started out two years before to find a child, we looked at domestic and international adoptions. Domestically, there are private adoptions where you pay to get a child or state adoptions where you don't. International adoption is costly, and the cost varies by country. We had zero funds for adopting, but I didn't want to adopt through the state foster care system because—I am ashamed to admit—I didn't want to deal with what I imagined were other people's troubled kids.

For more than a year, we hoped somehow to amass $20,000 to $30,000 to adopt internationally. I found Ethiopian children could be adopted for $16,000, and there was a volume discount—the more you adopted the cheaper they were. Racism and ableism played a hand in the supply and demand of adoptable babies. White children without disabilities cost the most.

My attempts at getting the money turned comically desperate. I tried winning $10,000 from *America's Funniest Home Videos*. I had submitted a tape of our German shepherd, Walt, playing tetherball. It wasn't completely ridiculous; he got air like Tony Hawk. I was confident he would have beat out the ubiquitous toddler hitting his dad in the nuts with a bat. While I did get a contract, he never made the final cut, and I realized I had pinned too much hope on this scheme.

One morning in April 2008, while still in bed, I turned to Ward and said we should adopt through the foster care system. No revelation. No real epiphany. It was a totally pragmatic decision. We wanted a kid, and the state had free ones.

"Sounds good," Ward responded.

Ward is like the Gary Cooper of husbands, which can be maddening when you want to talk about something but awesome when you just want to get on with it. The next month we went to an informational meeting on state adoptions at DHHS, and we got on with it.

To get a child from DHHS, you have to attend twenty-four hours of classes, twenty-three hours of which are basically designed to scare the crap out of you about the prospect of adopting a child in protective custody. Our instructors, Doris and Susan, were both mothers who shared their personal horror stories of trying to parent their "damaged kids" who were adopted from foster care. They also provided numerous examples gleaned from years of anecdotal-evidence gathering that sounded like plot lines from *Law & Order: Special Victims Unit*.

By the second night of class, it was clear these women wanted to prepare us for the worst kid we could ever imagine. They were real buzz kills when it came to getting in the dreamy parenting mood, and I wondered, *Is this really the way to market these kids? What about playing up the resiliency of the human spirit? Did these kids know this is how they were being portrayed? Could they sue for defamation of character?*

Halfway through the classes, I reached my limit of hearing about the killing of yet another family pet at the hands of a crazed eight-year-old or how you can love your little adoptive kid all you want, but if he has RAD (reactive attachment disorder) there is nothing you can do to get little Charlie Manson to love you back. In fact, your attempts at loving him might be met with resentful anger. I was glad we were hopeful to adopt a toddler because I figured I had a good chance of surviving an attack by someone under three feet tall.

I shared my fears with Ward, and he felt the same way. During the next class, we divided into small groups, and I took the opportunity to poll my group of prospective parents on their thoughts, whispering because I didn't want Doris or Susan to know I was questioning their tactics.

"Hey, I have a question," I said. "Is anyone else freaked out about all this killer-kid stuff?"

Charles, who stood about 6 feet 2 inches, weighed 190 pounds, and had three biological kids, said, "God, I can't take it anymore! I'm having nightmares!"

"Charles, be cool!" I looked over my shoulder to see if Doris or Susan were on to us.

The consensus with the others in the group was the same: what had we gotten ourselves into? Ward and I agreed this was our path, based solely on financial reasons, so I needed to make this okay in my mind. I started searching online to see if this anecdotal information was borne out in any data. I began with high profile cases of children who killed their biological parents. I also searched "adopted children killing their adoptive parents." In reality, kids had a greater chance of being killed by their adoptive parents. And, overall, children are less likely to kill their parents, biological or adoptive, than be killed by them.

Before class that evening, I presented my findings to Ward, which I had titled the "Menendez Theorem." I told Charles as well because he seemed so much more distraught than any of us. For the remainder of our classes—whenever Doris or Karen told a particularly chilling tale—Ward and I took turns whispering out of the side of our mouths, "Menendez."

During another class, we were instructed to create a family profile that could be sent to DHHS workers throughout the state. The profile was essentially a marketing tool to engage a worker on our merits as prospective parents, or as Karen explained, "Adoption staff are overworked. No one will contact you. You contact them."

A perky lady in our class who wore matching pastel-colored sweat pants and hoodies got the jump on all of us. She brought in a marketing confection she had whipped up overnight: handmade, colorful, laminated bookmarks with her family's profile on it, employing both text and photos. She had pulled fluffy yellow yarn through a perfectly punched hole at the top.

I hated her. What if this junior Martha Stewart got *our kid* with her artsy crafty ways? Where once we were all classmates, we were now future adoptive parents in competition with each other. There were only so many kids, only so many caseworkers, and only so many ways to set ourselves apart from each family.

As we set out making our own family profile, Ward was not as taken with the homespun, laminated bookmark route as I had been. Using standard white 8½ by 11-inch paper, Ward wrote our family profile, adding a few photos of us. Our introductory paragraph was basically our elevator speech: "We are looking to share our forever home with a 3-to-7(ish) boy of any race or nationality whose parental rights have been terminated. We have never been parents but we are very happy, excited, and committed about changing that situation."

Let's break down some of that description.

- "our forever home"—That's the terminology used in adoption and genuinely what we were offering, but it also sounded a little like *Grimm's Fairy Tales*.
- "a 3-to-7(ish)"—7(ish)? It sounds like an invitation for drinks at the Algonquin Hotel with Dorothy Parker, but the recommendation from class had been not to limit our options with regard to age.
- "whose parental rights have been terminated"—This meant the child was legally free for adoption.

After our graduation from class, we were sent out to find a foster care worker. We emailed our family profile to workers in all the counties of Maine, and a few leads came from those mailings. We were invited to a Foster Care Meet-and-Greet Mixer. This antiquated term should have been updated to Speed Adoption because it was an attempt to pair foster kids with potential adoptive parents in a short amount of time.

The event took place on a Saturday at an elementary school about an hour away. All prospective parents were gathered ahead of time in a conference room on the first floor. It became clear why we were all meeting beforehand: they didn't want any of us to screw up.

Ginger, who was one of the foster care workers, stood before us, clipboard in hand. "We have a group of kids in foster care here between the ages of seven and fifteen . . ."

A guy jumped in, "We're looking for a baby or a toddler at the oldest."

"Then you should probably leave now," said Ginger.

He and his wife quietly left.

"You can play basketball or make arts and crafts with the kids," she told us.

Ginger set her clipboard down. Her voice turned hard. "Do not spend too much time with any one child. It will give false hope. And do not tell any kid you are going to adopt him or her."

The last one got a chuckle from most of us, but not from Ginger.

"That's happened more than once. It seems like a no-brainer. Someone gets caught up in the moment, and a kid gets their heart broken."

It was then I realized this day wasn't just about us and what we wanted. As we filed out to go to the gym, I turned to Ward and said, "Maybe we should leave."

He continued walking. "No. What if our son is here?"

The kids were waiting when we walked in the gym. Some were looking at the floor, others seemed distracted by something on the wall, and a few looked directly at us. One of the dads in our group got the ball rolling.

"Who wants to shoot hoops?"

Ward went to play basketball, and I headed to the art table. Almost immediately, a boy about eleven or twelve years old sat next to me.

"How many kids do you have?"

"We don't have any," I said.

"I got a brother," he said motioning to where they were playing ball. "He's nine. We want to be in the same home. We're in different foster homes now but we want to be adopted together."

I wanted to continue staring at my hands but instead turned to look at him.

"Of course you do. That would be the best. . . . Don't you want to hang out with him?"

"Not today."

Of course not. Today, he was auditioning for the role of a lifetime. Ward and I had already decided we were not equipped to parent more than one child. As quickly and respectfully as possible, I moved to the other table. I found myself sitting next to an adorable girl who looked about seven. She was personable and funny, and I wondered how I could convince Ward we wanted her. My emotions were all over the place: stricken with heartbreak by the boy's story and then filled with excitement at the thought I may have met my daughter.

"What's your name?" I asked.

The girl turned toward me.

"Emily. My mom is Ginger," motioning to the caseworker at center court. "Our babysitter is sick today."

Well, there was no way I could disappoint Emily or get her hopes up, I thought.

I stayed with her and made a sock puppet. When Ward joined us, I again suggested we leave, and this time he agreed.

On the way to the car I said, "I can't do it this way. It's somehow too personal. That's a funny way to think of it but . . ."

"No, I get it. I feel the same way."

The months that followed could best be classified as excruciatingly close calls and near misses of other children we had heard were available for adoption but turned out not to be. In each instance, the caseworker we talked to would offer some tidbit regarding the child: he kicked a puppy; he's emotional; he shouldn't be in a home with other children; or he's been in three other foster homes.

The most painful situation happened over the course of a few days via phone conversations with a caseworker in another city. On a Wednesday, she told us about a six-year-old boy named Ryan. On Friday, we agreed to take him into our home the following Tuesday, which isn't as outlandish as it sounds—we had friends who got a call at 2:30 P.M. and by 4:30 that day a four-year-old girl was living with them. So we called family and friends to share the exciting news.

On Monday, the day before he was to arrive at our home, we received a call. A terrible mistake had been made. Another caseworker, who had seniority, had placed Ryan in another home over the weekend. If it's possible to have a miscarriage in the world of adoption, this was ours. I had to remind myself what a DHHS veteran told me: "You get the one you're supposed to get."

After four months of disappointment, frustration, and heartbreak following our classes, we still had not been able to get an actual sit-down with a foster care worker, so face-to-face time became our singular goal.

During the course of yet another conversation about the process, my sister, Betty, offered a much-needed changeup.

"You need to be unconventional," she said. "These workers are mostly women, right?"

"Yes."

"What do women like?" she asked.

"I don't know, Freud, what do they like?"

"It's really so simple, Kari. They like sugar."

"Sugar?"

"Okay, this is what you do. Go buy some donuts or cookies and crash DHHS. Tell them you want to meet with a caseworker."

"What?"

"These women work in little offices or cubicles," she explained. "They have stressful, crappy, low-paying jobs and they want sugar."

"They'll think I'm a flake," I countered.

"They'll think you have sugar!"

"Are we seriously entertaining this idea?"

"We are."

"Let's say you're right," I said. "Won't they see through this charade?"

"Kari, they want sugar, okay?"

"Okay, what should we get?"

"Dunkin' Donuts Munchkins," she advised. "The fifty-count box."

"Shouldn't it be something fancier?"

"Why put on airs?"

I decided not to overthink it. I called Ward and said we were crashing DHHS after work with some kind of sugary treat. I knew he was as beaten down as I was when he simply said, "Right. See ya later," before hanging up the phone.

As we were waiting in line at Dunkin' Donuts, Ward asked if we should get coffee, too.

"Betty didn't say anything about coffee. Let's not improvise."

With a box of Munchkins in hand, we stood in front of the DHHS building and reviewed our strategy. I squeezed Ward's hand and told him to follow my lead.

The reception area was in a small atrium. There was no mistaking the place for anything but an administrative building, yet there were attempts to be welcoming—the quilts hanging on one wall were made of squares that were reproductions of children's drawings. In the waiting area, twenty people sat on plastic chairs. A few people slept or had their heads down while others read the paper. No one smiled, let alone laughed; it was quiet for a room full of people. I started getting cold feet.

I turned toward the woman sitting behind the reception desk. She smiled and waved as we approached. She reminded me a little bit of Glenda the Good Witch. I took that as a sign the Munchkins were a good choice.

She cocked her head and a mane of blond curls spilled over her shoulder, "Can I help you?"

I put the box of Munchkins on her desk and just went for it.

"Yeah, I hope so. We can't get anyone to return our calls about getting a foster care worker. We have been through your training and we want to adopt a kid. We think we'd be pretty good parents—of course we have a lot to learn. But, the point is we need help. There are Munchkins in here—it's an assortment box—you get six to make the call, and the rest goes to whoever comes down to talk to us."

She smiled and then laughed. "You're serious, right?"

"Yeah, we are," I assured her.

Still laughing, she picked up the phone. Ward and I looked at each other and knew we were in. After she hung up, she told us someone would be down. She also asked if we would consider adopting her.

The woman who came down was Linda, the most awesome foster care worker, ever. She complimented us on our novel ways, and in the months that followed, she gave us some great advice, held our hands through this Byzantine system, and found us Thorin.

———

That first meeting with Linda was in September. On November 15th, I had a dream. I heard a voice say to me, "We found your son." I knew we had to hold tight. After we got Thorin, I would discover in his DHHS notes that the state's original plan of reunification had changed to termination of parental rights after his mother stopped visiting him. Their decision happened within a week of my dream.

———

On January 5th, Linda left that voicemail and put us on the road to Thorin. Three weeks after that, she sent me an email. The subject heading was empty, so I wasn't prepared when I opened it and saw the photo of Thorin. The text read "Here's a preview!"

"Oh," I whispered, "oh, look at you. You're absolutely beautiful."

I forwarded the email to Ward. While I waited to hear back from him I stared at Thorin and went through a half of box of tissues. I was struck by how much Thorin looked like Ward's brother, Andy: both had red hair and green eyes. It was the first thing Ward commented on when he called me a few minutes later.

"He looks like Andy!"

When I talked to Linda later that day I gushed, "Thorin is beautiful! And, he looks like Ward's brother!"

"Does he have Down syndrome, too?"

"No, he has red hair and green eyes."

Very emphatically Linda replied, "Kari, Thorin has blond hair and blue eyes."

"Not in this photo."

"Let me look, hang on a sec." After a pause she said, "You're right; it must be the lighting, but trust me, he has blond hair and blue eyes."

Hearing blond hair and blue eyes made me catch my breath. I was jolted into a forgotten memory. I cut the call short. On the first night Ward and I slept together, I had a dream. Like a film clip playing in front of me, I saw Ward holding a boy who was less than a year old. The boy had blond hair and blue eyes, and I knew he was our son. I didn't say anything the next morning. After a single night of passion, I assumed Ward would likely think I was Glenn Close in *Fatal Attraction* rather than Susan Sarandon in anything.

Now as I looked at the photo of Thorin, I knew he was the boy from my dream. Even though Thorin was two-and-a-half years old, at twenty-one pounds and thirty-two inches he would be mistaken for being much younger. I felt that calm again.

The photo was the only tangible evidence we had that Thorin existed. I carried him in my bag. I talked to him constantly in my head. Mostly, I said things such as "Hold on"; "Soon"; and "I love you."

Every couple of weeks, Linda would email with some new piece of information about Thorin:

- Thorin is signing the words "milk" and "more."
- Thorin went to Boston with his foster mom and another foster family to see the sights! He had a blast!

- Thorin had surgery a few days ago. Poor guy needed a root canal as well. They put him to sleep so they could do the work. Foster mom said he's been clingy but good-natured.
- Another family is interested in Thorin. They are from out of state and well off. My supervisor is insisting I consider them given the financial needs he will likely have. I'll call later.

The last update made me feel faint. I called Ward, and we agreed to ride this out. We had no other choice. We also wondered if Thorin needed a family with more money.

When I talked to Linda I told her, "We feel like he's ours. We want the best for him, but no one will love him more."

"I know that," she said. "Hang tough."

I had a dream a few days later. I was sitting on a chair in an otherwise empty room. I heard a voice say, "He's your kid." I stood up and left the room. When I woke up, I experienced that calm—my now familiar signal that it would be all right. I told Ward about my dream.

"Let's go with that," he said.

A week later, the other family had been dismissed as an option, and we were told we were the only family from here on in and the court hearing to terminate parental rights was a week away. Thorin would be "free" for adoption after that!

When the day arrived, there was a snowstorm that shut down the city and cancelled court. Linda called to let us know the hearing could be rescheduled in five to seven months. Until that time, Thorin would remain in reunification status.

"What does this mean exactly?" I asked.

"It means he is not technically free for adoption. Theoretically, his biological mother can continue to make a case for getting him back."

"In spite of everything . . ." I trailed off.

"I would call this a low-risk adoption," she said. "It is very unlikely he would ever be returned."

That's what every expectant parent wants to hear: "It is very unlikely he would ever be returned." Neither of us said anything for a moment.

"No one will blame you if you wait until the next hearing before taking him," she offered before we hung up.

My same friends—who had two hours to prepare for the delivery of their foster daughter—also experienced the painful reality of losing her. The little girl lived with them for nine months as they hoped and waited to adopt her, then she was taken away by the state and placed with biological relatives. States favor blood relations regardless of whether they are the best choice for the child. Four months later, the state returned her to them. My friends eventually adopted her, but not before all three of them had paid a hefty price. I knew it could happen us, too.

I briefed Ward.

"I would rather have him now," I said.

"She said 'low-risk,' right?" asked Ward.

"Right."

"I don't want to wait either."

We called Linda back and told her our decision. Our family profile of a boy whose parental rights had been terminated and who did not have a disability had gone to the wayside because of Thorin. We just wanted him.

●━━━

While most people meet their child for the first time in a delivery room, ours was introduced to us in the reception area of a single-story administrative building located in a business park alongside warehouses. Ward and I stood anxiously in the fifty-shades-of-office gray waiting room with Linda, Karen—Thorin's guardian ad litem (GAL)—and a foster care supervisor. It had been almost five months since Linda had told us about Thorin.

It wasn't too long before Sherry, Thorin's current foster mother, walked in with a very small boy in her arms. He peeked at us over Sherry's shoulder where he was burrowed. I can still see his profile against Sherry's sweater: a gorgeous boy with blond hair, blue, almond-shaped eyes, a little squished nose, and a shy, sweet smile. His soft fist was resting on his chin. Thorin became the subject in sharp focus, and everything and everyone in the room was a blur. I could hear appreciative murmurings faintly from the others.

What do you say the first time you meet your two-and-half-year-old kid? You want to say, "I love you! I can't believe this is happening!" But that, without a doubt, is going to freak out a child who has no idea who you are. Instinctively, Ward and I went to hug Thorin, which meant hugging Sherry too. We pulled both of them into us. We tried not to overwhelm Thorin, a difficult task when you yourself are overwhelmed. We didn't get to exactly melt into the moment as we hoped because were immediately ushered into a conference room.

The seven of us sat at a ridiculously large table for such an intimate matter. I kept my hands pressed against the table's edge, mostly so I wouldn't float away. For the first several minutes, everyone sounded like they were talking underwater. The blaring voice in my head drowned them out: THIS IS MY SON! THAT'S MY KID! I LOVE HIM! I LOVE HIM SO MUCH! IN FACT, I LOVE EVERYBODY!

How did they expect us to behave normally? Sure, doling out kids was old hat to them. In their minds, it must become procedural: "Okay, here's your kid you have been dying to meet. You probably haven't been able to think of anything else but this moment. But, please ignore your out-of-body experience; it's time to talk turkey."

Thorin started out the meeting in Sherry's lap. I was curious if Thorin was following the conversation. Did he realize the gravity of it?

The meeting started off focusing on why we wanted to adopt a child with Down syndrome. Karen, the GAL retained by the state to ensure Thorin's best interests were met, was fairly direct.

"Why would you want to do this? Why do you think this is for you?"

"We just know he's the one," I offered.

"Can you be more specific than that?" she asked.

"Well, it doesn't seem like that big of a deal . . ." I said, looking at Ward for more words. Being asked to defend why you want your child wasn't a normal question, it appeared, unless your child had Down syndrome. Why couldn't we love him freely without question?

Linda cocked her head in my direction and cut in.

"Susan, these are two educated and motivated people. They don't have other children. They could devote themselves entirely to him. That's what Thorin needs. Dedication. That's what they bring."

I had to admit that sounded pretty good—and frightening. The conversation moved on to how Thorin would be introduced to our home. Fifteen minutes or so into the meeting, Thorin edged out of Sherry's lap and moved to the table. He sat there silently then pushed himself the couple of feet over in front of Ward and me. He sat Buddha-like, moving his eyes from one of us to the other. It was clear we were being vetted. My first thought was "Our kid has serious balls!"

My love for Thorin had grown over the months leading up to that day. I was his mother when we walked through that door. Ward wanted him as much as I did, but I think he had not yet become his dad. That morning I watched Ward fall in love with Thorin. He held Thorin's small hands and beamed, then promptly and completely checked out. At one point, someone asked Ward a direct question.

"Listen," I said, "in case none of you have noticed, he's gone all daddy-o. I can answer for both of us."

After going over all the legalese and signing a million forms, Sherry and I set up the visitation schedule. We would visit him at her house over the next few weeks in preparation for him moving into our home. Our first visit would be the following day.

Once the logistics were covered, there wasn't anything else to talk about. Ward and I both tried to drag out the meeting with questions. It was as if we were on a terrific date and neither of us wanted to say goodbye. Linda took pity on us.

"I still have a little time. Do you want to take Thorin to lunch?" she asked. "Sherry and I can supervise."

"Yes! Great!" I said. I might have said it a tad too loud because Thorin put his hands over his ears.

"Why don't you two take him in your car?" Sherry suggested. "Linda and I can drive together."

She brought Thorin's bag and car seat over to us. Ward and I looked at each other. We had no idea how a car seat worked. Beginning when she was nineteen years old, Sherry had been a parent to over forty children—biological, adopted, and foster. She was in her sixties and found our lack of car-seat skills very funny. While she instructed Ward, I held Thorin easily against my hip with both arms around him. He looked up at me squinting.

"We don't know anything about car seats," I said.

Thorin nodded his head and yawned.

At McDonald's, we were chaperoned discretely. Ward and I sat with Thorin alone at our own table while Linda and Sherry sat a few feet away. Thorin was in a high chair, and we sat on either side of him. Most of our conversation was about food.

"Do you like the pickles?" I asked.

He shook his head no.

"Well, let's get rid of those, Buddy," said Ward as he pulled them off.

"Do you like ketchup?" I asked.

He nodded yes.

"Lots of it then, right?" said Ward.

"Kari, is that you?" I looked up to see a donor from the film festival I directed standing in front of me. For some reason, my first thought was how I would explain we take our kid to McDonald's.

"I told Mel it was you," she said. "We never come here, but the grandkids love it. What can you do, right?"

"Right," I said.

She stood clearly waiting for an introduction.

"Shirley, this is my husband and . . ."

I was stumped.

I stood up and put my hand in front of my face so Thorin couldn't see and whispered ever so quietly, "And this is our son who we just met this morning and are adopting."

She screamed. Thorin and Ward jumped in their seats.

Linda shook her head, sternly making a cutting motion below her neck.

"Do you have pictures? A camera?" Shirley asked.

"No," I said as I shook my head.

"I'm going to go get my camera!"

I didn't look to see Linda's expression. I wanted photos of this day. We had been told not to bring a camera. To Shirley's credit, she tried to be discrete.

"I don't want to overwhelm him," she said. "Oh, he's adorable. I could just eat him up!"

When we left, Sherry walked alongside Ward and Thorin. I hung back with Linda explaining to her my interaction with Shirley. She cut me off.

"Don't say that."

"Say what?" I asked.

"Don't say you're adopting him. He's not free for adoption, not technically, anyway."

I hated hearing that.

"What should we say?"

"Say you are his foster parents."

My heart sank. It sounded so impermanent.

Ward and I said goodbye to Thorin in the parking lot. The urge to hug and kiss him was great for both of us, but how would he feel? So instead, we both waved wildly, which I am sure was no less weird.

"See you tomorrow! We can't wait to see you!"

When we got home, I was happy to see Betty and her husband Matt on the front steps. The beauty of having your sister live next door to you is that you know you are going to run into her at some point during the day. She jumped up to hug us.

"How's our little man?" Betty asked. "Are you just over the moon?"

She and I started crying. Ward and I filled them in on the entire meeting.

"Everyone is going to want to hear about this tonight," she said.

By "everyone" she meant the other members of our apartment triplex. Betty and Matt lived next door to us in the same apartment as Johannah and her four-year-old daughter, Ella. On the other side of them were the McGirrs: Jimmy, Shonë, and their three-year-old daughter, Evvy. We had a common backyard where we ate together at least once a week in the summer and alternated apartments the rest of the year. Daily, there was a steady running back and forth between the apartments to visit.

That night we all met out back for dinner and discussed what was needed to make the little room next to our bedroom into Thorin's room. We had resisted making the transition until we knew he was moving in because we hadn't wanted to walk by an empty child's room for months on end. That night, Ward and I stayed up late talking about Thorin. We were in agreement he was the most-best-greatest kid, ever.

***

It took almost an hour—mostly on country roads—to get to Sherry's house. We waited at the top of the stairs to her deck. We waited because we didn't know how to operate a child gate. On the other side of the gate was Thorin and another boy we knew to be his foster brother, Jacob. Jacob was careening like Mad Max in a little push car. Thorin, who could not yet walk, was crouched on all fours scooting like a little monkey across the wood panels of the deck. Jacob came within an inch of knocking Thorin over. Ward, the soon-to-be-father of Thorin, yelled helplessly from behind the gate.

"Hey, slow down, Buddy . . . um, be careful . . . watch it!"

Sherry stepped onto the deck with a cup of coffee in her hand.

"It's okay, Ward," she said dryly. "He'd hit Thorin if he wanted to."

Seeing Thorin was still dreamlike and surreal. Ward and I looked at each other; this was going to be a long three weeks of visits. I wanted to hold Thorin. I wanted to hug and kiss him, but it seemed best to let him play.

Out of Thorin's earshot, Sherry said, "He's trying to figure it out: who both of you are."

She also filled us in on a few things about Thorin.

"He chokes a lot. Just make the pieces of food small. . . . It's always a good idea to stay calm when it happens. . . . You'll learn to understand what he wants. Talking is not the biggest obstacle to understanding him. Be patient. . . . Oh, he loves SpongeBob."

During our visit, Sherry suggested we take Thorin and Jacob to the pond at the end of her road. Jacob walked alongside Thorin's stroller, pointing out the landmarks on the way.

"That's the Harris's. They have a dog named Grover like from *Sesame Street*."

Thorin would nod his head and smile.

Once we got to the pond, both boys wanted their shoes and socks off. Jacob had his off in about two seconds. He then walked into the water.

"Hold up," I said.

"Jacob, you can stay in if you hold my hand," Ward added as he kicked off his shoes. Jacob was happy to comply with the offer.

Sitting on a little incline, Thorin pulled at his shoelaces.

"I'll help, okay? . . . Do you go in the water, too?" I asked.

Jacob answered for him, "Hold both his hands though."

I put my hands out in front of Thorin. "Ready?"

He grabbed my hands and pulled himself upright. We walked to the edge of the water.

"Do you want to go in?"

Thorin shook his head, no.

We stood together watching Ward and Jacob throw rocks they had pulled from the bottom of the pond. As we were getting ready to leave, I noticed the heel of one of Thorin's socks was muddy. So did Jacob.

"Sherry's going to know we had our shoes off," said Jacob.

"What do you mean?" I asked. "You're not supposed to have your shoes off?"

"No, go in the water," he volunteered.

"Ward!" I yelled. "Did you hear that?"

"Relax," he said.

I looked at Thorin. "I suppose you knew, too, right?"

Thorin smiled up at me.

"You're afraid of Sherry! You're afraid of Sherry!" sang Jacob.

"Settle down, Jacob," Ward said then turned to me. "Don't worry, Kari. We'll explain exactly what happened."

Sherry was fine with it all, and Jacob got the talking to, not us.

For two weeks, we would drive after work for an hour to Sherry's house, bringing dinner for everyone. It seemed like the least we could do since she was giving us a son. During each visit, we observed a little more. Thorin was feisty and curious, but his mood could turn somber quickly; it seemed he was both burdened and unburdened by his fate. It was clear he trusted Sherry, often seeking her help and approval. He loved her; I could see that by how he looked at her.

It was clear she felt the same way toward him. Sherry wasn't like a used car dealer trying to get a clunker off the lot. She was like a Porsche dealer wondering if we had the goods. Sherry could have put the kibosh on the whole thing if she had determined we weren't "the ones." Thankfully we proved worthy to her.

During one of the visits, Ward and I sat close on the couch with Thorin leaning back into both of us. His legs splayed over each of ours. We discovered he liked his feet massaged. When we stopped he would make the sign for "more," which he did repeatedly.

Sherry would indulge and encourage us. "Oh, there's something you know about Thorin I didn't. He loves a foot massage!"

Each night, Sherry would stay in the living room and allow us to give him a bath and put him to bed. The first night, we debated how much water was safe to use.

"That's not enough," Ward said. "I think that would be an unsatisfying amount."

"Listen, let's err on the side of too little tonight," I countered.

We saw Thorin sitting on the bath mat with his head in his hands. We were going about this all wrong.

"How's this look, Thorin?" I motioned for him to look in the tub.

He pulled himself against the tub and looked in. We got a big smile. I was going to help him in, but he stopped me. He shook his hand back and forth.

"Hah?" he asked.

"Hot?" Ward clarified.

Thorin nodded yes.

I put some of the water in a plastic cup. Thorin very tentatively put his index finger in the cup but just barely. He pulled it out dramatically and said, "Hah!" We found after a few more attempts of adding cold water Thorin liked his water tepid.

Before we left to go home, we looked into his crib and said about a million times, "We love you."

I am not sure what he thought when he looked up at us. He was more serious during these moments than earlier in the night. His gaze alternated between a hard stare and a furrowed brow. He was taking the greater risk here. He risked not only his heart but also his survival. Maybe he even thought, *Could these two smiling geeks pull it together and do right by me?*

Sherry allowed us to take Thorin a week before we had planned. She had been through this routine thirty-seven times before with other children. She knew the signs.

"I can see it. He's getting confused where he should be. He doesn't know if he is here with me or with you two. That's always a sign. Better get him home."

Two days later, we did. Sherry had made arrangements for Jacob to stay with a neighbor when Thorin left the house. They had said their goodbyes earlier in the day. None of us—Sherry, Ward, or myself—said anything as we moved from the house to the driveway with Thorin's belongings. Ward carried a box with his clothes and some toys. Sherry held his Playskool Sit 'n Spin.

Now it was time to leave. I held Thorin in my arms. We stood in a half circle next to the car, and it was difficult to know what to say. We had all prepared him as best we could, letting him know he was coming to live with us. But, this wasn't the time to remind him where he was going or to tell him his new bedroom had freshly painted yellow walls, a braided rug, and a lamp with the shadow of a sleeping cowboy. This night was about leaving Sherry.

The three of us had tears in our eyes. Thorin's eyes were dry, and he was silent. I saw a look, a brief flash that he knew his life with Sherry was ending. Ward moved to the front seat to drive, and I sat in the back next to Thorin. We made it to the end of the driveway and then Thorin . . . let go.

His sobs were painful and angry. It was unbearable. He raised his arms above his head and brought them crashing down on the arm rests of the car seat. He repeated this gesture until he slumped into his seat. Ward and I looked at each other in the rearview mirror. I tried to comfort Thorin by putting my arm around him, but he shook me off. I moved my hand to the seat between us.

I quickly realized you can't say to someone whose life you have just upended, "You can trust us," and expect their agony to subside.

So, instead, I said over and over, "It's okay. It's okay. It's okay."

His crying became like a scream. I had a knot in my stomach. I could see Ward's shoulders were stiff and tight.

"Should I pull over?" he asked.

Pull over to where? To where it wouldn't hurt anymore?

I told Ward, "Keep moving."

I started looking frantically through my purse for something. Anything. I saw one of my business cards, pulled it out, and turned to Thorin.

"It was so great to meet you. I hope we can keep in touch after the conference. Please take my business card."

I handed the card to him. Still sobbing, Thorin took it.

From the front seat, Ward said, "I don't mean to be critical . . . but that seems, maybe, not right."

I kept up the chatter, "Oh, it's just been great getting to hear your ideas. I hope we keep in touch."

Thorin eventually stopped crying and handed the card back to me, making little talking sounds. I didn't question it. I just kept it going. For that long hour drive, we handed the card back and forth and communicated that we wanted to stay in touch.

CHAPTER TWO

The Longest Labor

Ward and I wondered what we should expect when we brought a two-year-old foster child with Down syndrome into our home given we had no experience with two of those descriptors. What was unexpected was how low Thorin's Down syndrome ranked in our list of immediate concerns. Of the three—foster child, toddler, and Down syndrome—his diagnosis was dead last.

When the day came for Thorin to move into our home, we were immediately overwhelmed. All first-time parents are. If you're not, you're either doing it wrong or have an excellent supply of tranquilizers, in which case, you're doing it wrong.

Most first-time parents get to ease into toddlerdom. For the first year or so, parents are trying to get their kids to either eat or sleep—and trying to sleep themselves. We had to figure out those things and a few others, plus he came to us already mobile—highly mobile. He couldn't quite walk on his own—he needed only a bit of support to move around upright—but he was an accomplished crawler. Toddler-proofing our home consisted of seeing what he could reach, grab, or knock down and not putting things in those spots.

We had to learn not to react to alarming actions he made, if we didn't want him to do those things again, such as pretending to choke. He had quickly figured out choking scared the crap out of us. Do you know how hard it is to act calm while your son pretends to choke—or at least you're 85 percent sure he's pretending?

As new parents, we also got tons of advice, sometimes unsolicited, including advice we could not easily object to as parents of a child who was a ward of the state. The most adamant directive we received from Linda, Karen, and Sherry before Thorin moved into our home was "You are not allowed to have your foster child sleep in your bed." It wasn't like I wanted him to sleep with us; in fact, it never occurred to me. But, it was the first of many distinctions we would learn between being a parent of a foster child and an adopted child.

"It's not a good idea in general anyway," said Linda. "You could roll over and accidentally smother him."

Smother him! I wanted to say if I was going to accidentally smother anyone it would be our then aged mini-dachshund, Coco, who had halitosis and incontinence and farted nonstop. But, we did solemnly agree: no sleeping in our bed!

Three hours and twelve minutes into parenting, our solemn oath flew out the window. Thorin woke up screaming. We stood over the crib trying to soothe him, but he kept bouncing back up and yelling.

"Ow! Ow!"

"I think he means *out*," Ward said looking at me.

Vigorous head nodding and a big grin from Thorin confirmed that was correct.

"Well, it isn't like he can tell anyone we let him sleep with us, right?" I offered.

More positive head nodding came from our coconspirator.

Without further encouragement needed, Ward lifted Thorin from the crib, and the five of us piled onto the bed—two adults, one kid, a mini-dachshund, and a German shepherd—and slept through the night. From that moment on, we treated our foster child like he was our child.

The next morning upon waking, I realized, *Holy crap! We're parents!* I was beyond thrilled, but we now had an awesome responsibility. Seeing the rest of the bed was empty, I discerned Ward had gotten the household in motion already. When I came downstairs, I found Thorin sitting on the couch. He stared at me as he rubbed the sleep out of his eyes. He was wearing a onesie with little yellow fireman's hats on it that zipped from his left leg up to his neck. He sat in the lotus position, which impressed me because I was incapable of such flexibility. His chin rested in the cup of his hand, his elbow planted on his thigh. He gave an incredibly big yawn for such a small boy. I was on the verge of bursting into tears but knew that would be the wrong message for this auspicious morning, the beginning of our lives together.

Crap! I am going to completely lose it here. Think smaller. Think breakfast.

I turned my intense emotion of love into enthusiasm.

"We're so happy you're here!" I said, hoping I could keep it together.

Thorin offered a shy little smile.

Good grief! Everything this boy does is adorable.

After taking the dogs outside, Ward walked in the room. He looked at Thorin and asked, "You like eggs, right, Buddy? Sherry said you like eggs."

Thorin looked up at us and smiled. We took that as a yes.

While Ward made eggs and talked to Thorin, I went upstairs and cried into a bath towel. The months of waiting for a child had been all consuming. There had been no space for the unknowing of what it means to be a parent, and, at that moment, it hit me. I'm someone's mother. I do have an awesome responsibility. Not awesome meaning totally cool, but as it was originally intended: reverent, fearful, wonder. As the tears flowed, I pictured throwing myself in front of the proverbial bullet, car, or bear.

I heard Ward call for breakfast. I dried my eyes and threw the towel in the hamper. I walked down the stairs, secure with my new place in the universe.

The three of us sat at the table eating scrambled eggs. I had placed a miniature fork at Thorin's plate, but he used his hands to put little piles of eggs in his mouth. Ward and I were finished with breakfast in about ten minutes. At that point, Thorin had barely put a dent in his. Thirty minutes later, he was just halfway through his breakfast. I didn't want to rush him. Who knew what could cause him to choke?

As we waited for Thorin to finish, Ward and I ran out of conversation. Sitting at the table quietly gave me a moment to think about Thorin's hair—the extent of my parenting ideas at that moment. He had a butch haircut, which I thought was a shame because his hair was a brilliant gold. Where Sherry must have seen a miniature Army recruit, I saw Laird Hamilton, the big wave surfer.

"I bet you would look great with long hair," I said to Thorin. I turned to Ward, "Right?"

Neither of them said a word. Ward was minimal in his conversation, and I understood about four words Thorin spoke. I wondered if I would be talking to myself most of the time.

A knock came at the backdoor. I was grateful for my sister and Matt initiating the morning ritual of visiting Thorin. Three minutes later, the entire triplex was in our apartment to greet Thorin on his first day.

We decided a good after-breakfast activity would be to have Thorin explore the backyard with the help of a walker we brought from Sherry's house. There was a concrete path that ran along one side of the triplex, across the back, and up the other side. Both ends had gates that opened to the sidewalk. He walked from one end of the path to the other more than once, which was good exercise and preparation for walking.

The following morning after breakfast, Thorin pushed his walker to the backdoor where he made the sign for help.

"Ow! Ow!" he said, pointing to the backyard.

Ward carried the walker down the steps while Thorin crawled down backward. The scraping sound from the walker brought Ella and Evvy out of their apartments to visit. After Thorin's morning constitutional, they hoisted him up on the hammock, and the three of them swung back and forth. I felt comfortable enough to go inside and do the dishes.

A few minutes later, Evvy ran into our apartment.

"Thorin and I kissed each other!"

"Oh my!"

"I guess we're getting married," she said as she twirled around the kitchen.

"You know, I don't think you have to go there yet."

Shaking her head she replied, "If I marry him he has to stop wearing sweat pants and T-shirts all the time."

I laughed, "Men in general don't like to be told what they can and cannot wear."

Crinkling her nose she said, "I think I should talk to my mom about this," and ran out the door.

Hearing Thorin's biggest obstacle as a marriage partner might be how he dressed was awesome, as in totally cool. As Evvy went flying down the back steps, Betty and Johannah arrived.

"We're going to throw you guys a toddler shower," Johannah told me as they walked in.

"Is that done?" I asked. "You know, in this kind of a situation?"

They both laughed.

"Won't people think we're angling for free stuff?"

"I hope so," Betty said. "Set up a Target registry."

Three days into our parenthood, the phone rang. It was Linda.

"Hey, I wanted to give you all a chance to settle in before I told you about some things that are coming up fast."

She rattled them off like a grocery list:

- She would be visiting us once a month.
- Karen, Thorin's GAL, would visit once a month.
- Thorin's sister Jade, who lived in another foster home, wanted to see him.
- Thorin would have weekly visitation with his biological mother.
- A preschool had been chosen for Thorin, which he would start later that week.

As I was frantically writing it all down, I realized Linda had no idea what "settle in" meant. My immediate concern was the weekly visitation with his biological mother.

"I thought this was a low-risk adoption?"

"It's still low risk," she said. "But, his biological mother hasn't lost her rights at this point. She's entitled to see him. She's also entitled to go to doctor appointments."

"Does he see her alone?"

"No. The visits are at DHHS. They will be supervised by a caseworker. You'll bring him and drop him off."

We first heard about Jade a couple months before Thorin moved in. By all accounts, Jade was described as heroic. After Thorin was born, she often stayed home from school to make sure he was cared for and safe. She became more than his sister; she became his caregiver because the adults in the house weren't capable. As Thorin's health deteriorated, Jade realized she needed to get him help. On separate occasions, she notified a teacher and a staff person at the neighborhood police office about what was happening in her home. No help came. Finally, she went directly to the police station to report her family. She was ten years old.

Thorin was taken to the hospital where he recovered enough to return home. State mandates were created to keep families together, which is great if the parents get better at parenting. Back at home, his health started to decline again, and he was placed in protective custody.

For that first visit with his mother—Thorin had been with us only a week—I prepared him as best as I could. We had told him we were "Mom" and "Dad," but did he know what that meant? We had no idea what he thought about the dramatic changes in his life.

"I'm taking you for a visit with your . . . biological . . . mom," I said. "Sound good?"

No response from Thorin.

"It's a short visit. It'll be in an office. You've done this before, right?"

He sat on the couch, impassive.

"I'll be there to take you home after, okay?" I added, "I'll pick you up and bring you here. I'll bring you home."

Thorin hadn't lived with his mother in almost a year and a half. I hoped he would take his cue from me, so I decided to project that this was not a big deal. That would be the message. I would lie.

I dressed him in a recently purchased outfit from Target I had earmarked for special occasions. I imagined it was something he would wear to meet new family: green khaki shorts, a yellow and green plaid short-sleeve button down shirt, and a khaki hat with a yellow stripe band. He looked adorable. I pulled him onto my lap and held him and gave him extra kisses before we left the house.

When I walked through the doors at DHHS, Glenda the Good Witch, whose name I learned to be Patty, waved us over.

"Hi, Kari! Hi, Thorin! Good to see you, little man!"

"Hi, Patty!" I looked around trying to figure out which of the women sitting in the waiting room was Thorin's mother.

Patty shook her head. "She's waiting for him back there," motioning down the hall. "And this is Michael," pointing to a man walking toward us. "He'll supervise. Michael knows Thorin from other visits."

Thorin almost jumped out of my arms to hug Michael, and off they went, just like that, with no backward glance at me for reassurance. I looked at Patty, who was staring at my chest. I looked down and saw I was holding the front of my shirt over my heart tightly.

"Try not to worry," she said. Her phone rang. She looked sad as she answered the call.

I knew I couldn't sit in the waiting room for the next ninety minutes, so I decided to go home. On my way, without thinking about it, I pulled into a gas station and bought a pack of cigarettes. I hadn't been a regular smoker for twenty years. At home, I sat in our backyard and smoked one cigarette after another. I was numb and dizzy, which was preferable to the emptiness I felt as Michael walked away with Thorin. When it came time to leave, I washed the bitter smell off me, ran water over the remaining cigarettes, and threw them in the trash.

I returned to DHHS and walked into the lobby. Michael was standing next to Patty, holding Thorin in his arms.

I reached out to him and asked, "Hey, Sweetie. Ready to go?"

Thorin snuggled into Michael more. I was the odd man out. I was the interloper. Thorin knew Michael longer than he knew me. I had loved Thorin for months before we had met, when he didn't even know we existed. I was crushed and didn't know what to do.

Michael gently pulled Thorin away from his chest, "Airplane, Dude?"

Thorin put his arms out to his sides. Michael held him lengthways from underneath and flew him toward me. Just as he would get near me, Thorin would shake his head and pull back his arms. After a long, three or four minutes, Thorin let himself fly into my arms, and we headed back to the car

"How did it go?" I asked from the front seat as I was driving home.

Thorin stared out the window, ignoring me.

A few days after Thorin visited with his biological mother, we toured the preschool picked for us. We were completely underwhelmed when we went for a visit. It had an institutional vibe: 1960s school tile, harsh overhead lighting, and tight quarters. The classroom was a combination of gray, tan, and beige. It wasn't *One Flew Over the Cuckoo's Nest* but it didn't scream preschool fun either. It was hard to picture Thorin, who was lively and vivacious, being happy there. I said as much to Thorin's case manager from child services, who we met for the first time in the hallway. Kimmie looked like she was twelve years old.

"This is the best place for him," she told me. "Trust me."

Weren't there enough people in our lives? Now added to the mix was a school director, a school case manager, a special education teacher, an aide, an occupational therapist, a physical therapist, and a speech therapist. A couple days before Thorin started school, Ward and I attended our first Individual Education Plan (IEP) meeting. An IEP is a legally binding document that lists the special accommodations a child with a diagnosis needs to participate in school. Later, I came to think of it as "the meeting I try not to cry at" or "the meeting I try not to lose my shit at." IEP meetings are unnatural. The process goes against every parental instinct to shield your child from criticism, judgment, and inspection.

I didn't know any of that, though, when we sat down with a room full of strangers for the first time to figure out what Thorin needed. After introductions were made, the case manager for the school asked each person to recommend what amount of service Thorin should receive.

"Let's start with you," she said, motioning to the physical therapist. "How much time for PT?"

"One hour should be good for right now," she answered.

"Okay, speech?"

"Can you wait a sec?" I interrupted. "One hour a week for PT?"

She looked up from her note taking and smiled. "Yes."

In unison, Ward and I said, "He can't walk!"

"You two sure are on the same page!" she said laughing. "That's pretty standard though."

"Okay, what does a kid who can walk get?" I asked.

"It isn't about him walking or not," she said. "It doesn't work like that."

"How does it work then?" Ward asked.

Kimmie spoke up, "It's great you're advocating for Thorin but . . ."

"We want more than an hour," I said, cutting her off. "How do we make that happen?"

This was the process for each service: they offered something, and we said it wasn't enough. The school director attempted to lighten the tone of the meeting.

"We're looking forward to Thorin being here with us. He's such a charmer, and what a beautiful child."

"I know!" I said. "I would love to get him into modeling."

No one said anything. Complete silence. Alice suggested we move on to coordinating Thorin's school hours with my work schedule.

The classroom teacher was the last to speak. She described the daily routine and introduced the concept of "typicals" to us.

"The typicals will see him at free play," she said. "We'll send a typical into the classroom as a model for him and the others. If we send more than one typical into a classroom, they tend to stick together, so it's better to just send one."

"What are *typicals*?" I asked.

There was an awkward silence.

Ward turned to me, "They're the ones who don't have Down syndrome."

"Not just Down syndrome," she said. "Any child who's disabled."

As we drove home after the meeting, Ward said, "Isn't that just fucking typical?"

Laughing, I responded, "Those poor bastard typicals."

Neither of us said anything for a few minutes.

"Is 'disabled' the right word?" questioned Ward.

"What about me bringing up Thorin modeling?"

Ward cracked up.

"Kari, the looks on their faces! It's like you said, 'I'm going to teach our dogs how to tap dance!'"

The next week, Ward met Thorin's mother when he took him for his cardiology appointment. Thorin had two holes in his heart. This appointment was a checkup to monitor his condition.

Ward called me at work when they got back home.

"Good news! An ultrasound revealed no holes. That means both holes have closed!"

"Really?"

"Yes, really. We can cross that off the list for him," he said.

"What a relief!" With hardly a pause, I asked, "What about *her* being there?"

"She held him, undressed him, and changed his diaper in the office. I didn't want her to feel short-changed out of her social time with him," he replied.

Ward had empathy for her that I couldn't seem to muster. To me, she was the enemy.

"She answered some of the questions about him while the nurse was there," he said. "She knew more about his history, but when it was about how he's doing now, she started to answer and then kind of got quiet, so I stepped in."

"How was Thorin?" I asked.

"He was friendly with her," he said. "But, she demonstrated so little curiosity about how he's getting on. I don't know if it's that she doesn't want to acknowledge her lack of guardianship or that it doesn't occur to her to ask. On the bright side, awkward silence is better than an awkward conversation."

———

Thorin's next blast from the past was his sister. Linda called and said Jade wanted to see him, so we made arrangements with Jade's foster family to get them together. They had only seen each other once in the last year and a half. On the drive to her house, we explained to Thorin we were going to see Jade. Thorin's face lit up. He hugged his chest.

Jade's foster mother opened the door and ushered us in. Jade walked toward us, and I was struck by how small and unassuming she seemed. From what I knew of her, I thought she would be taller somehow or would look like Wonder Woman. Thorin was beaming. We briefly visited with her foster family before she left with us to go to lunch.

At first, Jade didn't want to order anything, insisting she wasn't hungry, but we convinced her to order a burger and fries. Thorin sat in a high chair next to Jade, who cut his grilled cheese sandwich into tiny pieces before she started on her lunch. He watched her intently, smiling.

"Do you both work?" she asked.

"We do," said Ward.

Then a serious vetting session ensued: What did we do for work? How long had we had our jobs? What was our education? Why didn't we have children? Why did we want to be parents? It was clear she wanted to know if her brother was being treated well. One thing she didn't ask about was Down syndrome.

We must have passed the test because the conversation moved on to favorite movies and books. Then we all smelled "it."

"He needs his diaper changed," Jade giggled.

Ward grabbed Thorin and the diaper bag and headed to the restroom. This was my chance. I had to know how a child becomes heroic.

"Jade, how did you go to the police?"

I knew she didn't understand the intent of my question when she answered, "I walked there."

"You're brave," I told her.

"Yeah, I hear that a lot."

After Ward and Thorin got back to the table, I switched topics, and we set up another date for the following week.

———

The toddler shower fell on the month anniversary of Thorin living with us. Over thirty people came, including Ward's family from New Jersey and New York. We got everything on our list—which Johannah, who had been a parent for more than four years, had helped us create. My contribution to the registry was a request of Andy Warhol's portrait of John Wayne to complete Thorin's western-themed bedroom.

We also received two of the greatest inventions known to humanity: the Pack 'n Play and the Diaper Genie. If you had asked me even a month before the shower to name the greatest products ever invented, neither one would have made the top 1,000. Of course, that was before I tried to take a shower while alone in the house with Thorin or held a poopy diaper and an entire pack's worth of dirty baby wipes, wondering if I closed the gate at the top of the stairs as a half-naked kid crawled down the hall.

Whatever reservations people had about Thorin having Down syndrome were replaced with welcoming him to the fold. He was held and kissed by one and all while Ella and Evvy showed him off.

"Yeah, he knows how to sign and he can say, 'What's that?' Go ahead, Thorin, show them," said Ella about thirty times during the party. He obliged to squeals of delight and clapping.

Ward's sister Carolyn brought her three children. The youngest, Benny, was fifteen months old, which made him seventeen months younger than Thorin. Benny was built like a linebacker for the Green

Bay Packers. He was big for his age, but it was striking to see how tiny Thorin was next to Benny. Carolyn brought Benny's hand-me-downs, but Thorin wouldn't fit in any of the clothes for a couple of years.

That day, there was more than one sidebar conversation out of Thorin's earshot about his status as our son. It was confusing to people, and explaining that was difficult.

"But, he is yours, right?" one friend asked.

"Not exactly," I said. "He isn't free for adoption yet. We're waiting for a court date."

"You're going to leave it to fate then," she said.

"No, not fate. He's our son. We wanted him to move in rather than wait."

"If it's meant to be, it will be, right?" she said with a wink.

I wondered how she would feel if someone said that about her child.

"This is how we got him. He's our son with a stipulation we've accepted."

"I guess I don't understand that," she said, sounding angry.

"That's the best I can do today." Now I sounded angry, too.

That night sitting in the backyard, I shared my frustrations with Betty.

"People have such small ideas about parenthood," Betty said. "She can't see you feel the same way about Thorin as she does about her kid."

●━━━

The beginning of the next month was the kickoff for Linda's and Karen's home visits. Linda was easier to have at the house. She was tough and nosey but also funny and smart. Most of her comments were about what a good job we were doing.

"How long is he in that?" Linda asked, pointing to the Pack 'n Play.

Ward looked at me and winked, "No more than five or six hours a day?"

I laughed.

"Don't joke with anyone else like that. You would be surprised how humorless some people are," Linda advised.

Enter Karen, Thorin's GAL. Nothing was funny to her. She was a lawyer paid by the state to represent Thorin's interests. Ward and I were in this limbo existence where his mother was making a case for getting him back although she wasn't following through on stipulations set for her. Karen could stand in the way of us keeping Thorin if she advocated for Thorin's biological mother over us. She also seemed obsessed with Down syndrome.

"I'm sure you've considered all the things he will not be able to do," she said.

Thorin was sitting in the middle of the coffee table playing with a Curious George stuffed animal.

"No, we haven't. Who knows what anyone is capable of? Everyone has strengths and weaknesses."

"What a nice way to look at it," she said smiling.

It seemed pointless to explain I wasn't being nice.

Karen was also a proponent of the "people with Down syndrome sure are happy" mindset. Here, she was not alone. One of the most prevalent stereotypes about people with Down syndrome is that they are always happy. The inference here is "these people" are so blighted their personalities are flatten to a single non-discriminating emotion. Until Thorin moved in with us, I had forgotten I had known someone with Down syndrome.

I was thirteen and two weeks away from my Lutheran confirmation. Without talking it over with my parents, I visited with Pastor Larsen.

"I don't believe in God, so I can't get confirmed," I told him. What I didn't say was that church seemed judgmental to me.

The pastor gave me reasons to get confirmed anyway, including, "You're thinking about the whole thing too much. I'm positive there are other kids who feel the same way."

"So it's up to them to say something or not, right?"

"That's not what I meant," he quickly replied. "No one in my thirty years of being a pastor has ever refused to be confirmed!"

My parents were furious. Not so much for the overthinking religion part but for the embarrassing them business. We agreed they would not drag me by my hair down the aisle of the church to be confirmed, and I would volunteer at the church rather than attend the services. My job was to help in the basement with the "retarded kids" while their parents attended the church service. It was a small group of children who had Down syndrome.

The room had dark wood paneling, brown carpeting, and a large table with chairs. There were no toys, construction paper, or anything for a child to play with. I immediately hated the adult volunteer who ran the little gulag. He seemed to get off on how pathetically hopeless he found the children and how great he was for spending his time with them.

"They're hopeless. We don't do much here but make sure they stay in the room," he told me on my first day.

I nodded, wondering why these kids couldn't be in the regular daycare—my younger sister was on the second floor of the church in the daycare room, likely eating paste. However, one of the kids was not a kid. He looked to be in his twenties. Even as a teenager, I was very much aware he was an adult. His name was Monty. He wore a green suit with a striped tie; his shoes were shined, and his hair combed back. He was dressed for church. In spite of his circumstances, he presented himself in a dignified manner, sitting at the table sipping from a glass of water. I hoped his impassive gaze toward the center of the room was a mask and inside he was able to spirit himself away to another place.

I lasted there one more week. At thirteen years old, I had no idea how to change what seemed so obviously awful to me in that basement.

The first time I heard the word *happy* in reference to Thorin was about a week after he moved in. I was unbuckling him from his car seat when a neighbor came up behind me. He hadn't met Thorin officially but he had seen him.

As he looked over my shoulder at Thorin, he said, smiling, "They're always happy, aren't they?"

I knew he wasn't talking about toddlers in general, but I didn't know what to say. It was like I was in the church basement again.

———

Two months into parenting Ward notified me that he wanted Thorin to like him best.

"What the fuck does that mean?"

"I want to be the favorite. There's always a favorite parent, and I want it to be me. You're bossy so it isn't like you'd stand a chance anyway."

You can learn a lot about someone when you start parenting with him. My once noncompetitive mate was now actively campaigning against me in the likability department with our son. When I shared my frustration with Sherry, she responded practically.

"Good! Their fun time away from you is your alone time."

And, it didn't help that Thorin refused to call me "Mom." He called me "Ba" and Ward "Daddy," or sometimes "Mommy." Thorin even called the mail carrier "Mom" eighteen months before me. I was an inarticulate syllable, and Ward was a fully articulated word commonly used for someone in a parenting role or a character in a Tennessee Williams play.

Did it bother me? Yes, it bothered me. Sure, I was gratified by the stories of other mothers who told me about how daddies are always the favorite. I had more than one friend suggest Thorin was doing it to bother me.

"No shit!" I responded on all occasions.

However others parsed his decision—and I do believe it was a conscious decision on Thorin's part—I wanted to hear that word in relation to me. It was important to me, as it would be to any mother.

———

At one of our visits at DHHS, I unexpectedly met Thorin's biological mother at drop-off. I came through the door, holding him, and saw a woman talking to Michael. Michael gave a quick wave, and she turned toward us—my nemesis.

I walked toward her in what I hoped was a normal gait rather than what felt like staggering forward. We exchanged brief pleasantries. Then the three of them walked away. I called Sherry when I got home.

"I'm terrified we're going to lose him," I said.

"It's an awful thing waiting," she said. "It's just awful. If you can, don't give in completely to him. Protect yourself."

When I returned to DHHS, Thorin's biological mother had already left. I went through what now had become a ritual of the airplane game to get Thorin back in my arms. I asked Thorin how he was as I pulled out of the parking lot.

Nothing. Never anything. He stared out the window.

I asked if he wanted to go for ice cream. He made two thumbs-up in the backseat. No discussion necessary; we both liked ice cream.

⸻

A few days later, Ward and I had been copied on an email from DHHS that included an email from Don McCreedy. I found out from Linda he was the state's attorney handling Thorin's case. He would be arguing that Thorin be freed for adoption. His role was not ambiguous.

"I should talk to him," I told her.

"No, you don't need to do that. Besides, he's very busy," she said.

After I hung up, I immediately emailed him. I didn't see the point in trying to convince Linda what I was doing was okay.

Dear Mr. McCreedy,

I wanted the opportunity to formally introduce myself to you. As you know, we are Thorin's foster and hope-to-be-adoptive parents. We love Thorin. We can't believe how lucky we are to have him and very much want to keep him. I would like to know how I could help make that a reality. I am sure this is a bit unorthodox and I know you are terribly busy.

Look forward to hearing from you!

Kari

I hit the send button and waited. Less than twenty minutes later, he emailed back with his phone number: "Please feel free to call me."

I made sure Thorin couldn't hear me and was totally engaged with SpongeBob when I made the call. The biggest piece of information was that this was not a slam dunk.

"I want this as much as you do," he said. "That said, there's no guarantee."

"She hasn't done anything, the court said . . ."

"Yeah," he replied, "but the burden is on the state to prove its case, and it is a high standard to meet. Terminating parental rights is a very serious thing to do. The state must prove the birth parents' unfitness above all, and, secondly, that termination is in the best interest of the child."

"What can we do to help?"

"Take good notes. Document everything," he said. "Be good parents. That'll be easy."

"How strong is the case?" I inquired.

"Good case."

"Okay then. Thank you for talking with me."

"You and Ward have the heavy lifting. Call or email me whenever you want." Then he paused. "You're going to hear this from Linda, anyway. . . . The court date is definitely not July."

I couldn't keep the disappointment out of my voice. "Why?"

"One of the witnesses has a family obligation out of the country," he explained. "He is available by phone, but the mother's attorney is fighting that. The judge will probably agree with her."

"So when?"

"It could be September."

"Could it be sooner?" I asked knowing that was unlikely.

"It could be November," he said making me feel worse.

———

In spite of the uncertainty, we couldn't help enjoying Thorin. He made the stress and fear worth it. Part of the fun and struggle was getting to know each other. There were the typical barriers to learning about your child plus others. We didn't really speak the same language. He could for the most part understand me but couldn't tell me what was on his mind. We didn't know each other's likes or dislikes.

I think some of my early bonding with him started in the grocery store. I like to eat while I shop. I picked up this habit from my dad. Not thinking one day, I opened a bag of Cheetos and started eating. Thorin made the sign for "eat," so I gave him one of the Cheetos. By the time we got to the checkout, our hands and lips were covered in that weird Cheetos orange. I knew I was going overboard but I didn't want to stop. I was the fun parent for a change.

The cashier commented, "Oh, look at you two and your orange faces!"

Thorin and I gave each other a high-five.

Cheetos became part of our regular shopping experience. During one shopping trip, a lady who looked like the kind of mother who monitored television watching and cooked nutritious meals was walking toward us in the diaper aisle. I almost closed the Cheetos bag and shoved them under the other groceries. Thorin and I had Cheetos in our hands, gritty with orange dust, when she reached us.

"Those aren't good for him," she said.

"I know, but he's addicted to them."

He and I cracked up. He didn't understand what *addicted* meant but he did think I was funny. It was this cosmic moment where we got each other. I was a parent! Did I wish I had more to offer than crappy foodstuffs and wisecracking? Sure. But it was still an awesome thing.

———

I received special permission from DHHS to take Thorin to Wisconsin to see my mom. She had visited us the month before to meet Thorin. The trip turned into a six-day lovefest because they spent most of the visit cuddling. My mom was finally becoming a grandparent at seventy-seven.

Never having traveled with a child, I was overwhelmed by what I needed to carry: food, toys, paper, crayons, markers, diapers, wipes, a change of clothes, and a travel stroller. And then there was my stuff. Thorin and I took a shuttle bus to Boston Logan International Airport. When we disembarked, I had to quickly learn how to push a stroller and pull a suitcase at the same time.

I had a terrible fear of flying. My routine was to sit next to the aisle for easy escape when the plane went down. It was great if I could get my seat partner to keep the shade down. Otherwise, I kept my eyes closed and pretended I was on a bus. Thorin, who had never flown, had other ideas: he pushed the shade up and looked out the window. I couldn't keep my eyes closed because I was a parent now.

On the first flight of our trip, we ran into the most terrifying turbulence I had ever experienced. Thorin was actually bouncing above the seat; he loved it, laughing hysterically and making the sign for more. I turned to look at the guy across the aisle. He was watching Thorin with a huge grin on his face.

"Kids, right?" he chuckled.

The connecting flight required us to go through security, again. We were stopped by TSA.

"Ma'am he has to walk through the scanner."

"What? He can't walk," I said. "I don't understand."

"You can carry him then."

The alarm went off.

"Ma'am, take his pants off, please," the TSA agent said. "And remove your barrettes."

I stood numb.

"Ma'am, his pants have metal on them, and your barrettes," the TSA agent said, motioning to me.

The line behind us backed up as I unhooked Thorin's overalls while holding him and pulling the barrettes out of my hair.

"Ma'am, hand me your bag. We need to search it."

"Ma'am, are you sure he can't walk through?"

"He can't walk."

I watched as some conferring between the TSA agents ensued. Then I noticed a group of young men who I guessed were Indian. One of them stepped forward.

"Why are you doing this to a baby, sir?" he asked the TSA agent.

You could have heard a pin drop.

"Sir, you need to get back in line, now."

I turned and mouthed "thank you" to our fellow traveler. I felt the same as our defender. I knew it was wrong but I wasn't going to win against TSA.

"Okay, you can carry him through," the TSA agent said.

After I went through the scanner, two TSA agents laid Thorin down on a stopped conveyer belt and patted him down. They lifted his thin sweater and T-shirt. They opened his diaper, looked inside, and reattached it. They went through everything in our bag, placing the objects on the belt. They tested the liquid in his juice container.

When they were done one of the agents said, "Okay, you can go."

I felt like we had been beat up.

"They're jerks," the woman behind me in line whispered in my ear. "What gate? I'm going to get you there."

The woman helped me repack my bag and dress Thorin. She walked us to our plane and gave us both a goodbye hug. I couldn't say anything to Thorin. I wanted him to think it was a normal occurrence. During the flight, I felt sick about what had happened. I knew it had to do with Down syndrome somehow because in our short time with Thorin most things people did that were rude or offensive had to do with Down syndrome.

My mom picked us up at the shuttle station. She and I started crying. She held Thorin as she hugged and kissed him.

"I missed you so much, Thorin!" she told him as he burrowed into her neck stroking her hair.

Then she offered him ice cream.

"Mom, it's dinnertime."

"Why can't we have ice cream for dinner? Right, Thorin?"

Thorin responded with two thumbs-up. I was outnumbered.

Later in the evening, my mom informed me she had bought an inflatable mattress—for me. Thorin would sleep with her in the bed. As I tried to get comfortable in the living room, I heard them giggling. Then Thorin would sigh, followed by murmuring and more giggling.

At breakfast, my mom announced she wanted to show off Thorin to everyone. Our days were filled with visits to relatives and family friends. She also brought Thorin to cocktail hour in the great room at her senior living complex; the joint was rife with grandparents.

"May I present the best grandchild in the world!" she told the assembled group, which stopped all conversation. Then my mom whispered to me, "I think they're shocked at how beautiful Thorin is."

"Well," I whispered back, "they're shocked by something."

One morning while Thorin slept in, my mom told me about a couple who lived on another floor. The previous week, she had found out they had had a granddaughter with Down syndrome who died when she was five years old. The wife had wanted to share a photo of her granddaughter with my mom.

"I never show her picture to anyone because I don't know what the person will say."

She and my mom looked at the photo. My mom commented how pretty her granddaughter looked. They also talked about Thorin. During our stay, I ran into the husband taking my mom's trash out. He introduced himself to me by saying his granddaughter had Down syndrome. Before I could say anything, he continued.

"We loved her. We didn't care that she had Down syndrome. None of us did. She lit up our lives. You know what? No one ever said congratulations when she was born. Not one person. Then she got sick. She had a bad heart. It killed me when she died. Twenty-four years ago . . . I still miss her every day. You know what? People said things like it was a blessing but it wasn't; it was awful."

My eyes were wet. I looked up at him. His powerful arms were crossed tight against his chest straining his shirt. His hard eyes said it all: "Don't hug me and don't cry. I can't handle it." Then he walked away.

When we first heard about Thorin having holes in his heart, I did research. I discovered on the Global Down Syndrome Foundation website that "up until 1984 doctors in the United States refused to provide lifesaving procedures to people with Down syndrome such as surgeries related to the heart. Even today, there are people with Down syndrome dying in their 30s or 40s simply because a doctor refused to perform . . . heart [surgeries] when they were infants."

The conversation I had that day with him took place in 2009. His granddaughter died twenty-five years before that, making her death sometime in 1984. I knew I could never ask him what his family had been told. From his deep grief, I'm convinced it wasn't—your granddaughter is not worth saving.

The night before we left to go back home, my mom and I sat in her living room while Thorin slept in the bedroom. We reminisced about our short trip and talked about when she would be able to come to Maine. She also shared something that had been bothering her.

"How did I think he was going to be so much work? Why did I think he would be so different?"

"It's okay," I said.

"It's not," she replied. "I'm disappointed in myself. All those months I feared him, I could have just loved him. I will never forgive myself."

We sat quietly.

"It'll work out," she said. "This time is your labor."

"Labor?"

"You don't get a child without experiencing great pain. For you and Ward, this time waiting for the court date is your labor."

If I had known what having a child would do for my relationship with my mother, I would have had adopted one when I was twelve. Thorin created a profound and unforeseen change in the nature of our relationship: we both loved the same person with such intensity our love aligned us in a way like never before. She was no longer the mother, and I was no longer the daughter. Now she was the grandmother, and I was the mother. I would later get into the habit of calling her while I waited during Thorin's visits with his mother. Sometimes we talked about where he was, and sometimes we talked about anything else but that.

On the flight back, Thorin and I were put under the same scrutiny by TSA. This time I couldn't hold in my feelings. As the woman lifted up his clothes and padded his diaper, I let the tears fall without wiping them away.

"I love children. I do. I have a niece and a nephew," she said, trying to convince me.

In disbelief, I shook my head back and forth.

When I got home, I quizzed everyone I knew if they had experienced or witnessed such a thing by TSA. No one had. I looked online and came up with my best deduction: the year before in Baghdad, Al-Qaeda had strapped remote-controlled explosives to two women with Down syndrome that were detonated in a marketplace killing the women and scores of others. Had the TSA agents seen other parents with their children as normal families on their way to visit grandparents and me as a mad bomber who would use her child as a weapon simply because Thorin had Down syndrome?

One of the perks of being in Wisconsin with my mother was that I missed both a visit with Thorin's mother and a visit from Karen. They both brought up very different feelings, but both represented threats to Thorin staying with us. If Karen had told us her report to the court would be favorable toward Ward and me, I could have accepted her. Instead, she was cryptic and said she hadn't written her report yet.

I felt powerless, impotent. When she visited the day after we got back, I had to keep my hostility in check because her job was judging our competency as parents. About ten minutes into the visit, she asked to use the bathroom. She routinely asked to use our bathroom, and I was convinced she was snooping.

Having read countless mystery thrillers, I knew if I placed a tiny piece of paper in one of the corners of the medicine cabinet I could tell if she had looked inside. After she left, I found my little paper trap had fluttered on to the floor underneath the sink.

I decided this indiscretion on her part deserved some response on my part. I knew she couldn't operate the child gate at the top of the stairs to the second floor where the bathroom was located. During her next visit, she asked to go to the bathroom, so I led the way upstairs to open the gate for her. Instead of leaving it unlocked, I quietly locked it back in place. Once downstairs, I took Thorin and the dogs outside. Almost fifteen minutes later, she walked out the backdoor. We were sitting on the patio, eating fish crackers and drinking apple juice.

"You couldn't hear me yelling?" she asked as she wiped sweat off the back of her neck.

"Yelling?" I asked. I hadn't actually heard yelling.

"I have been stuck behind that gate, yelling," she said. "I finally got it open . . ."

"I'm sorry."

"You didn't wonder where I was all this time?"

I shook my head. "Those gates are tricky. . . . Fish crackers?" I said, offering her the bag.

———

Our opinion of Thorin's preschool never changed. Ward and I were constantly meeting with the school's teachers and administrators, both separately and together. I was troubled by the fact his teacher was often holding Thorin when I came to pick him up. She would completely envelop him with her arms and lean over him with her body. I asked to speak with her and her supervisor. When she came to the office for the meeting, she had Thorin in her arms.

"Couldn't you have left him in the classroom?" I asked.

"He seems so happy with me holding him."

I looked to the supervisor for guidance, but she was smiling patiently for me to continue.

"He should be moving around and playing with other children," I said in an instructive tone.

The teacher looked up from Thorin and responded, "My kids really hate me. My husband and I are getting a divorce."

The supervisor shook her head sympathetically. I was speechless. Did she expect me to say, "Oh, by all means then please hold my son on your lap all day if it will make you feel better." I realized there was no point in continuing the conversation.

As I reached to take Thorin, I said, "Okay, you can go back and play with the other children." I carried him to the classroom and left.

A few days later, Ward called me at work, livid. "I just got a call from the physical therapist!"

"Okay."

"She's doing a report on Thorin. She hasn't had time to see if he can crawl stairs so she wanted me to tell her if he can."

"For Pete's sake! What did you say?"

"I told her that he can climb stairs. Then I asked if there was anything else she didn't get to."

We were concerned Thorin would not develop there, instead becoming more helpless. One day, I showed up a few minutes early at lunchtime. There were about eight kids and four teachers sitting around a table, eating. I saw an aide sitting behind Thorin with her arm around him from the back shoveling yogurt in his mouth. I made a conscious effort to be calm and maintain my composure.

"What are you doing?" I asked.

I thought what I said was in a sort of oh-so-curious tone. But, the look on the other kids' faces and the fact that some had stopped eating with their spoons in mid-air told me I had sounded more like Linda Blair in *The Exorcist*.

No response from the aide, who had pushed her chair back from him.

"He can feed himself," I told her. My disgust was clear.

Discussion of Thorin's preschool dominated our life. Ward and I talked about the school endlessly at night. I talked to my sister.

I talked to two friends at work almost on a daily basis—both were parents. After a while, they were all saying the same thing: "You don't like this place and you don't trust these people."

A few days later, I forgot to notify the school that I would be coming two hours early to pick up Thorin. As I walked down the hall to his classroom, I heard screaming coming from behind one of the doors—horror film screaming. My heart started racing. Without thinking, I opened the door. It was Thorin screaming uncontrollably as he thrashed in a chair, unable to move freely because he was restrained by a belt at his chest. His hair was wet and matted against his head. Sitting next to him, as if nothing was amiss, was a woman who was several months pregnant, reading a book.

I flew to Thorin, unbuckled the belt, and lifted him into my arms.

"What are you doing?" My voice was shaking.

"Speech therapy."

Really? Did she really think what she was doing was a therapeutic? I wanted to smash her.

"Why did you strap him in?"

"Because he tries to get away."

That stopped me cold. I should have called the police. Instead, I turned and left with Thorin. We were done there.

I called Ward.

"How many people walked down that hall and heard him screaming?" he asked immediately after I gave the play-by-play.

I wondered how many times she had done that to him before that day. When we reported it, nothing was done. It was chalked up to inexperience on the part of the speech therapist. What I saw was not inexperience but an act of cruelty. If I hadn't walked in on it, I would never have known because Thorin couldn't tell me.

It had never occurred to Ward or me that this type of treatment was possible. It was not on our list of worries as new parents. We worried about covering the electrical sockets, whether his car seat should face backward or forward, and if his food was cut in small enough pieces.

I would learn later that restraint was a common occurrence for children who have disabilities. A landmark study by United States Department of Education's Civil Rights division found 267,000 occurrences of restraint used at school in 2012. Three-quarters of the students were children with a disability.

Until we could find another preschool, I took Thorin to work with me. Most days we were alone. I was the executive director of a film festival and the only year-round staff person. It was a tough month for both of us. I put markers, books, movies, juice, and food in his backpack. They were not adequate distractions for an active two-year-old in a workplace environment. At some point, popcorn or Goldfish crackers—occasionally both—would be thrown at me. Juice spilled on the carpet or on Thorin. And then there was whining—from both of us.

I did not realize how stealthily and quickly two-year-olds could hatch escape plans. One minute Thorin would be playing quietly on the floor, and the next, boom, he would be gone. I almost always found him lying prostrate in the hallway surrounded by toys and food. Once—just once—a woman from another office found him at the end of the hall, pounding on the 100-gallon fish tank.

"Are you sure this is going to work?" she asked as she walked in my office with him in her arms.

"It is working," I said in a chipper tone. "Thank you!"

Could we have found a daycare? Maybe, but we were terrified to leave him with anyone except family and friends. We had already met the Boogeyman; he was a twenty-something pregnant lady who palmed herself off as a speech therapist. Anything was possible.

I tried to turn my meetings into phone conferences whenever possible. On one occasion, I hammered out the logistics of a film presentation at an elite college with a professor and the college's development director on the phone. I was engaged, informative, and witty. Basically, I was killing it. As the call continued, I saw Thorin holding up an empty wrapper of fish crackers, making the sign for more. I reached over, grabbed a bag, and tossed them gently to his feet. He couldn't open them. Before I could rectify the situation, he screamed.

"Baaaaaaaaaaaaaaaa!"

"What was that?" the development director asked.

"I don't know," I replied. "What did it sound like?"

The capper for me was the day three board members came to the office for a meeting. I had made arrangements for my sister to take Thorin for two hours, except she got sick with a stomach flu. *Oh well,* I thought, *they might as well meet my kid.*

I wore an oatmeal-colored linen wrap skirt and a white linen wrap blouse. Thorin sat on my lap while I printed the documents for the meeting. What I didn't realize was that he had untied both wraps. So when they walked in the office, and I rose to greet them, my skirt fell off and my blouse opened. *Really, he can't open a package of fish crackers but he can undress me.* No one said anything. I don't know if it was the harried look of a new mother on my face or the fact they could tell I might burst into tears, but everyone took their seats as if nothing had happened.

As summer wore on, I started to note changes in the nature of Thorin's visits with his mother. I would arrive and find that she had left twenty minutes early. After one visit, she asked me if he could nap before I brought him because he was very active. Why didn't she know a nap would make him more awake and active?

I realized even this limited time with Thorin was too much for her. I wondered if she knew she wasn't up to the task of running after an active and curious two-year-old. I was eleven years older than her and I knew how demanding the task was.

Twenty-five minutes into another visit, Michael called me to come back and pick up Thorin. It was 90 degrees and muggy. When I got there, Thorin reached out for me immediately rather than staying in Michael's arms.

"This guy was a little fussy. It's so hot in there. She cut it short. He was too much for her," Michael reported.

It was hard not to feel encouraged.

—

Our pretrial conference was at the end of August. When we arrived, Ward and I found Linda sitting on a bench outside the courtroom. We had been told by Linda the purpose of this proceeding was to set the court date for the determination of parental rights hearing—no decision would be made that day. The conference was scheduled to begin at ten o'clock; twenty minutes later, nothing had happened.

"These things never start on time," Linda said yawning.

A few minutes later, she was called into the courtroom. Ward and I didn't think anything was unusual because this was all unusual for us. But after an hour of various people going in the court room then coming back out, including Thorin's mother, it was hard not to think something was up. Then Karen walked up to us.

"Can we talk?" she asked. "There's a room down the hall. Linda will join us."

The four of us sat around a small table in a room no bigger than a vestibule.

"Things have changed," Karen said. "Thorin's mother is considering voluntarily terminating her parental rights today."

"I can't believe it," I said.

"What's happening?" asked Ward.

"His mother would like to continue visits," said Karen.

"No," I blurted out. I could tell Ward was nervous about my answer, but he didn't say anything.

"Would you send photos to her?" Linda asked. "It would be through our office."

"Yes," I said.

They sent us out into the hall. Thorin's mother was there; she didn't look at us. I avoided eye contact with her, too. Twenty minutes later, we all filed into to the courtroom. The judge asked her in several ways if she understood what she was doing. Each time, she said yes. She quietly cried the whole time, and Ward and I had tears streaming down our faces. My heart went out to her. In that moment, I could only feel gratitude. She was no longer my nemesis. She was a mother giving up her son for the right reasons.

She signed the papers and asked if she could leave. Thorin was ours.

Top: Thorin and Bubba; Bottom: Thorin calls me Ba

CHAPTER THREE

A Typical Son

As Ward and I drove from the courthouse to pick up Thorin from Shonë, we tried talking about what had transpired in the last hour.

"Do . . . you . . . you believe . . . what was," I stuttered.

"No, I could never," Ward said.

Alarmed I asked, "Did you just run a stop sign?"

"I'm glad you didn't see the first one."

"Maybe we should pull over."

We parked next to a grocery store for a few minutes, sitting in silence and staring out the front window into our future. Our lives were suddenly and remarkably different. For Ward and me, our experience of parenthood was no longer marred by fear and trepidation at the prospect of losing Thorin. For Thorin, it finally meant permanence: we were his forever family. I was relieved Thorin's painful origin story now had a happy ending.

When Thorin was old enough to understand, I would tell him his mother loved him so much that she made a decision that was difficult for her but was the best for him—that was objectively true. No matter what his mother had done or not done in the past didn't make her decision less noble. She was helping Thorin secure a better future.

When we walked into our apartment with Thorin, I went upstairs. I made it to our bedroom before my legs started shaking so badly that I dropped to my knees. I trembled and sobbed. The fear left me like a tumbling wave. I couldn't do anything but ride it out until it passed. After several minutes with my face against the cool hardwood floor, I was able to get up and behave normally again.

Ward and I took turns calling our family and friends to let them know that Thorin would always be their grandson, nephew, cousin, and friend. Saying it each time made it more real. This was our birth announcement, as much as his adoption ceremony would be eight months later.

We took Thorin to dinner to celebrate. He didn't know what we were celebrating exactly because we had shielded him as best we could from the unknown, or at least hoped we had. We hugged and kissed him throughout the meal. Ward and I would spontaneously break into laughter followed by tears. Thorin clapped wildly as he laughed. He made the sign for "more" over and over again.

Our conversation was a running loop, followed by Ward kissing me then Thorin.

"Thorin, we love you so much!"

"Thank you," he signed.

Our waitress asked, "Is it somebody's birthday?"

Looking up at her smiling, I wondered what she would say if I told her we were celebrating the birth of our family. Instead, I told her a close truth.

"No, we're just very happy to be together."

As I ate, I realized the tight band I felt across my chest for months was gone. My breathing was easier and more expansive. I felt buoyed and grounded at the same time. As I gazed at Thorin, I was struck how he looked to me. Like the first time I saw him, he was in sharp focus, and everything else was a blur.

Back home, we all fell into a sound sleep. At about three o'clock in the morning, I was awakened by a vivid dream: I saw calendar pages floating one after another like a clichéd film montage showing the passage of time. It was funny to me that the dream was so literal, but the sensation it raised in me felt like a great whoosh, pulling me out of bed.

In a still dreamy state, I went downstairs in search of my appointment book—I know that makes me a troglodyte. I flipped the pages backward until I found the day we had gotten the first call from Linda about Thorin. I then counted forward to the present; it was one day shy of nine months. My mom had been right. Our long labor had been the length of a pregnancy.

Three days later, Linda emailed to inform us that she and Karen would still be visiting until we could adopt Thorin, but their visits would be more *pro forma*. She explained we would be notified at some point of our adoption date and our status officially had changed from foster parents to pre-adoptive parents. We could make more independent decisions but we still needed to notify DHHS first. It was a parenting promotion.

The first order of business was finding a new preschool for Thorin. I couldn't continue to bring him to my office and actually get work done; plus he needed to be with other children during the day.

After some careful investigating, I located a school highly recommended by both parents and professionals and scheduled a tour. When we pulled into the parking lot, Ward and I found a single-story brick building with painted window sashes. The entryway was framed with a homey post and beam front. On both sides of the entrance, there were well-groomed shrubs along with some small trees.

At the door, Ward pulled the handle and discovered it was locked. To the left of the door was a keypad with an intercom. A cheery voice answered after Ward pushed the call button.

"Hello Pecks! I will be out soon!"

I wondered how they knew it was us, as I scanned the doorway for a camera. As we waited, Ward pointed to the twelve-feet-high enclosure with red and green playground equipment peeking over the fence on the other side of the parking lot.

"That's must be some playground! I'm liking what I see."

I tapped Ward's shoulder. "Hey, how can I make a surprise visit if the doors are locked?"

"Let's assume you won't need to carry out any surprise visits here, Kari."

The woman who answered the door was peppy and athletic looking. Her red shorts and green-striped polo shirt matched the building, making her look like an illustration in a children's book.

"I'm Louise, one of the directors of the school! Come on in!" As she talked, *The Love Boat* theme played in my head—she reminded me of Julie, the cruise director.

Our tour began in the spacious lobby. On one side, there were vertical, multicolored cubbies with coats and backpacks hanging inside. The other side had a large aquarium filled with exotic fish. Next to that was a bookshelf filled with both resource materials and children's books, and the far end was a glass wall that looked into the school's office.

"This look great!" said Ward enthusiastically.

"Thanks! Sorry about the door. We keep it locked after morning drop-off. Safer that way, right?"

"Can I drop by anytime?" I could feel a gentle nudge in my back from Ward.

"Of course! It'd be great if you let us know when you were coming, though."

"That seems more than reasonable," said Ward as he cast a look in my direction.

I narrowed my eyes; I knew I would most certainly not be giving them notice the first time I dropped by.

A staff person walked into the room wearing a headset. She smiled and then spoke quietly into her mouthpiece, "The Pecks are coming your way soon," after which she reached out her hand to shake ours.

Louise pointed to the windows and said, "We have blackout shades that we can deploy as part of our lockdown protocol."

"Seriously?" I asked.

"Yes," she replied. "We take safety very seriously. Unfortunately, the reality is school-place violence happens. Whether by noncustodial parents or even strangers."

I hadn't even thought about those possibilities and reconsidered my previous assessment, wondering instead if Louise was a former Navy Seal. As we walked down the hall after her, Ward whispered, "They have you beat in the safety department."

Louise allowed us to look into the classrooms briefly before moving on.

"We have an almost equal mix of children with and without disabilities. Thorin wouldn't be the only child with Down syndrome."

Ward asked, "How'd you create that ratio? Why would parents send their children here if they didn't have a disability?"

Louise smiled. "Some parents believe diversity of all kinds is important to their children's development. Also we have numerous siblings here. Parents want their children at the same school."

We filled in Louise on what had happened to Thorin at the other school. She didn't say much but she seemed attentive. She recommended Thorin have a tour before his first day at the school, so he would have an easier transition.

We learned that the chair Thorin had been restrained in was actually a therapeutic chair. The belt was designed to help children with low muscle tone. Cinched to the point of abuse was actually a manufacturer concern. Ward and I both noted a few of the chairs at the new school. I wondered how Thorin would feel about seeing them.

When we came back to the school with Thorin, Louise gave him the same tour, fortunately without noting the blackout shades or lockdown protocol. She focused on what he liked doing, what he ate for lunch, and his favorite color. When he signed "yellow," he was pleased to know she understood him.

Louise showed us a room that looked like a large closet, maybe five square feet. It was cramped and contained a small table with three chairs and shelves packed with games, puzzles, and books. Ward and I stood outside the room while Louise and Thorin went in.

"This is the speech room, Thorin. The door can stay open when you are in here, if you'd like." Then she pointed to a chair identical to the one used to restrain him. "Thorin, we cut the straps off this chair. Can you see they are gone?"

He nodded yes.

"Thorin, this is your chair. We've put your name on it, see?"

Thorin pushed himself upright against the chair to study his name written in marker on the back. He smoothed his hands over the frayed webbing left from the belt.

Looking at her, he signed, "Thank you."

It was hard to hold back the tears, but I did. Thorin was stoic about it, and I would be, too.

On Thorin's first day of class, I carried him into the building. He was not fearful but excited. Thorin gave me a quick kiss then went off with his teacher, crawling quickly alongside her. I saw other parents pulling their clinging children's bodies off their own so they could make their escape. I was relieved Thorin seemed happy to be rid of me. The alternative looked dreadful and undignified.

Thorin's physical development took off after he started at the school. In the previous months, we had encouraged him to walk, but he met us with what I thought was resistance. When I would see him take a step or two, I would get so excited and yell, "Great job, Thorin," which caused him to jump and hermit crab scuttle away from me, all the while looking over his shoulder. As we walked outside, I would suggest he touch my fingertips and walk, but he would drop to the ground and start fast crawling away.

I tried bribing him with animal crackers. Sitting on the couch, I said in a cheery voice, "Hey, Thorin, walk just this little bit to me, and you can have a cookie!"

No response.

"It's a lion!" I said followed by a roar. I had never faked roared in my life, and listening to myself, I realized even I wasn't buying it.

Thorin gave me a disgusted look then pulled himself up as he held on to the coffee table. He made his way over to me, never letting go along the way, smiled broadly, and put his little hand out to take the cookie. He bested me and he knew it.

I shared our adventures in walking with his physical therapist at the school.

"Thorin has low body tone. He needs to develop his strength so he can truly feel confident in supporting himself," she explained. "I know you think you're supporting him, but it might feel like pressure."

"Pressuring?" I immediately felt like Mommie Dearest. As I looked at her, I nodded affirmatively, but inside I told myself I was a fraud for not knowing what Thorin needed.

Forcing an energetic and grateful tone, I added, "Thanks for telling me this! I can dial it back and focus on what he needs."

"Sounds good!" she said.

"Terrific!" I replied. Once I had a few hours of distance from that conversation, I came to the realization I was not a fraud, just a parent on a learning curve.

Thorin developed his strength quickly with the physical therapist's businesslike instructions. In no time, Thorin was walking a few steps, falling, getting back up, and trying again. Ward and I held back on the overboard praise. One evening I told Thorin, using a normal tone of voice, that he was doing a good job walking as I pretended to watch Project Runway. Inside I was jubilant. Our pulling back made room for Thorin to show off rather than perform.

A few weeks later my sister, Ward, and I were sitting in a circle on the living room floor with Thorin.

"Hey, Buddy can you take two steps to me?" Betty asked.

Thorin pulled himself up and staggered over like Baby Frankenstein. We all offered subdued praise: "Nice job, Dude," or some variation of that was said by each of us. Then Ward asked Thorin to walk across the circle to him. The distance was four steps, which he handled like a champ.

"More!" Thorin signed excitedly.

The three of us casually spread our circle out to increase the distance he would need to cover.

"Thorin can you walk to me?" I asked.

He covered six steps to get to me. Thorin made whooping sounds at his destination, which was our cue. We cheered. Instead of retreating, Thorin clapped wildly. Next, he successfully tackled eight steps. We clapped exuberantly.

We carried on until he was too tired to continue. I lay on my back staring at the ceiling, grinning and holding Thorin close. I got to see my son walk for the first time. He was almost three years old—past the point of when typically developing children walk, but it didn't feel too late.

After that night, Thorin was able to walk unsupported unless the terrain was uneven or challenging in some way. Walking for Thorin was no longer a test but a way to get to some place more expediently.

His speech therapist, on the other hand, was not as accepting of Thorin's abilities.

"He's not where he should be," she said the first time Ward and I met with her.

Something about that phrase bothered me. It seemed Thorin was being blamed for something.

"Where should he be?" I asked.

"He should be better. He's so far behind; I don't even know yet."

Ward and I were still new to advocacy. Comments like these, shared by professionals about Thorin, were sometimes stunning, other times troublesome, and, thankfully, usually just annoying. The speech therapist's comments were troublesome because she might be translating these diminished thoughts into her practice in a way Thorin could internalize.

Early in our relationship Ward and I had bonded over the fact we both loved Walt Whitman's *Leaves of Grass*. Our love of Whitman even prompted us to name our German shepherd Walt. It was either that or live with the shelter's name for him: Shultzy.

As a teenager, Ward discovered the beauty of *Leaves of Grass* the same summer he discovered cunnilingus with his then girlfriend. Whitman would have been pleased, I'm sure. When her parents found out Ward had given their daughter a copy of *Leaves of Grass*— they called Whitman "a dirty poet"—he became *persona non grata*. I can only imagine what would have happened if both his discoveries were known to them.

My discovery of Whitman was less earthy. Twenty years before, I'd worked at a small, prominent college as a therapist. One of my clients was a nineteen-year-old returning to school after having a psychotic break. He returned home and saw a psychiatrist weekly. He was meeting with me as part of his transition back to school.

I learned he liked the psychiatrist but didn't think he was really listening to him. I also learned he came from a working-class family who saw him as the family hero attaining the unimagined: an education with the sons and daughters of the elite. His mother had already predicted the rest of his life. He would be successful, wealthy, and upper class.

"Do you see any obstacles to returning to school?" I asked.

"I have one. I want to leave school and play hockey in Europe."

"Oh boy, that's a big one."

"Yeah," he laughed at the enormity of it.

"When did you decide this?"

"In high school, but no one thought it was a good idea. Then the last year while I was home, I spent my days lying on a lawn chair in the backyard, daydreaming of living in Europe, being in a new city every day, and playing hockey."

I was thrown. I wasn't sure what my role was in his life decision. And, I wasn't sure I wanted his parents or the school upset with me. I shared all these details with my clinical supervisor.

"In contemplating the leaves of grass, he found his true nature," he told me.

"Right."

"He doesn't want to be here. Maybe his break was less psychotic and more of an awakening," he suggested.

On the way home, I stopped at a bookstore. That night, I cracked open *Leaves of Grass*. I immediately opened to the complete, perfect beauty of Whitman. For two days, I dog-eared hundreds of pages and highlighted countless lines.

"How good are you at hockey?" I asked the student in our next meeting.

"I'm here on a hockey scholarship."

"I guess you must be pretty good, then."

"This is possible! I have a friend over there now doing the same thing. The problem is what other people want me to do," he said, sounding tired.

During the rest of the session, we talked about following your dreams regardless of what other people thought. Three days later, he came to wish me goodbye. He had finagled passage on a cargo ship headed to Rotterdam. *How Whitmanesque*, I thought. The lesson I took from him was that not being where you should be—based on other people's estimations of you—was not a deficit; it was just another place.

There was plenty Ward and I didn't know about childrearing when Thorin arrived. And, there was plenty we didn't know about Thorin. Very early on, I became aware Thorin seemed to be able to read my thoughts. The first time it really struck me was when I had my back to him in the bathroom. I was washing my hands, and he was unrolling the toilet paper all over the floor. I distinctly remember thinking, *I hope he doesn't notice my keys on the tank and throw them into the . . .* splash! He threw my keys in the toilet!

There were several of these events where I would think don't do that, and, sure enough, he would do exactly that. Not having been a parent, I thought it was bonding process that occurred between parent and child. I talked to a woman in the neighborhood who had two children and did childcare in her home. I gave her a few examples of Thorin's abilities.

"It's strange, isn't it, how our kids can pick up on our thoughts," I said to her.

"Yeah, I've never heard of that."

I didn't have the bandwidth to put a lot of thought into these incidents at the time, what with everything else going on.

My energy was needed for everything else Thorin, especially communication. Our thinking was if he could be understood more, other things would fall in line. We didn't pressure Thorin to talk but we did expect him to try as best he could, which he did. We also didn't place a higher value on talking over other forms of communication. Thorin usually signed to communicate, but he would also spontaneously talk.

Walt, our seventy-pound German shepherd, was lying on the floor, and Thorin wanted to get by him.

"Get up!" yelled Thorin.

He was still less than two-feet tall, but Walt jumped up so Thorin could make his way. Then he complimented Walt, saying "Good Walt!"

Thorin also started telling me "good job" when I changed his diaper.

I shared these observations with his speech therapist. She nodded her head but didn't say anything. I didn't even get a smile. I wondered if she thought, *Poor Ms. Wagner-Peck . . . can't accept the fact Thorin isn't where he should be, so she makes up stories.*

This suspicion by professionals of the accuracy of what Ward and I reported as Thorin's development would continue over the years. If they didn't see IT personally, whatever the accomplishment might be, IT didn't exist. It was frustrating to be considered suspect by someone who saw Thorin only a fraction of the time Ward and I did.

Our communication challenges didn't interfere with the fact that I knew when Thorin was mad. He became more comfortable being angry with us—more specifically with me. When Thorin was with Ward, he mostly squealed with delight, but with me, it was a lot of testing behaviors. We had been cautioned in our classes about the honeymoon period that adoptive families experience. Some children who are adopted tend to stifle their natural developmental behaviors until they have assessed the adults' ability at coping.

Thorin started signing no to me upon any request I made, which was typical for a two-year-old child interacting with his parent. It annoyed me sometimes, but I took it as a healthy sign. It did get ridiculous when I would open my mouth and he would yell no before I could say anything.

He also regularly pulled shenanigans to assess my temperament. One morning, I turned my head just in time to duck before getting hit in the head with an open container of applesauce. It decorated the wall behind me, making a drippy mess.

"That didn't look like an accident, Mister. Did you mean to do that?"

Thorin gave me the thumbs-up sign.

As I cleaned up his mess, I could hear him snickering. A few minutes later, he threw his juice on the floor. Thankfully, it had a top on it. This type of behavior became common at most meals.

Ward, on the other hand, found parenting a breeze—primarily because he was most comfortable in the realm of fun stuff. I had to deal with the actual responsibilities of parenting: transporting Thorin to and from school; meeting with staff at the school; buying clothes, toys, and books; and dealing with the mostly typical behavior meted out by toddlers.

At least a few times a week, I would ask, "Can you say Mommy, Thorin? Can you please?"

"No, Ba," he said, shaking his head vigorously.

Thorin's rebuff reminded me of a story that one of our adoption class instructors had told about her adopted daughter. For ten years, the girl addressed every birthday card to her in the same way: "Happy Birthday, Mrs. Clifton!"

I took two things away from that story: it gave me hope that the girl used an exclamation point, and I remembered Mrs. Clifton saying not to take it personally. I would eventually figure out that most of parenting was not taking things personally.

In the outside world, I also was often not acknowledged as Thorin's mother. My age caused this confusion, and I struggled to not to take it personally. Soon after Thorin started preschool,

I argued with a five-year-old who insisted I must be Thorin's grandmother.

"Really, with all that gray hair?" he countered.

"For your information, it's platinum," I retorted.

"Yeah, right."

On another day, I walked out our front door with Thorin in my arms, looking, I thought, hip and youthful in my dark rinsed jeans, my short-wasted safari jacket, and my black cat-eye sunglasses. As we made our way to the car, a man about my age passed by.

"Are you the grandmother?" he asked.

My cover was blown.

"No, I'm the old mother," I said breezily.

During those months before we officially adopted Thorin, I turned fifty. It was not a traumatic event; it was a cakewalk, in fact. With all the things related to being new parents, Ward forgot I was celebrating that seminal birthday. No one else remarked on it either. I was not the recipient of the longstanding tradition of black birthday balloons or not-so-funny cards commenting on my advanced age. I realized that my mid-life crisis looked like what most people do with the first half of their lives. I was literally flipping the script.

———

Sherry notified us that Thorin's former foster brother, Jacob, was being placed with a family in town, and he would soon be attending the same preschool as Thorin. The boys had only seen each other one time since Thorin moved out of Sherry's house. I knew Thorin missed Jacob. Someone had given him the book *The Snowy Day*, where the central figure is a young African-American boy. Whenever I read it to him, Thorin would press his hands over the boy and say "Jac-ub."

When the boys saw each other again in the hallway outside of their classrooms, Jacob said hi to Thorin and reached toward him. Thorin was smiling brightly. They gave each other a light pat on the arm. Then they spent part of the morning playing together.

The relationship was not an easy one for Thorin to continue. When they lived with Sherry, they were the only children in the house; they were each other's playmates. At school, Jacob had his pick of many children to play with. He was also able to talk, walk, and run and had the strength to explore the entire playground.

I was told by staff every once in a while Jacob would play with Thorin in the sandbox, happy to hang out with his former foster brother. I asked Thorin if it bothered him.

"No, Jac-ub good."

⸺

Thorin's propensity to throw food, drink, and objects increased in occurrence and location. He was doing it at home, others people's homes, restaurants, and school. We bestowed upon him the nickname Throwy Peck. Throwy was a bit of a misnomer. Aside from throwing, he could reach over and ever so lightly knock over his juice or milk.

My response to this behavior alternated between ignoring it, pretending it was an accident, yelling, and, while ineffective, crying over spilled milk. For a while, I thought maybe it was Pavlovian. What was troubling was my belief that he was training me with the unconditioned stimulus of throwing things to elicit a conditioned response. How frustrating for him that I kept changing my reaction.

⸺

Ward realized I was doing more than my fair share of parenting—after I told him every day for months. There were gaps in Thorin's preschool hours, and I couldn't fill them all. Four days per week, Ward started going into work early so he could take off Thursday afternoons to be with Thorin.

On one of their Thursdays, Ward and Thorin were downtown when a woman panhandler asked Ward for spare change. He handed her a couple quarters. What came next was wholly unexpected.

"Is his name Thorin?"

Ward was taken aback. "What?"

"Is his name Thorin?" she repeated.

"How do you know him?"

"I'm friends with his mother," she answered. She then looked at Thorin, who was staring at her.

"You don't remember me, do you?" she asked.

No acknowledgment came from Thorin, and Ward continued walking forward, cutting off any more conversation.

"It's good you got him! You're doin' a wonderful job," she called after them.

This encounter would not be the last time we would run into someone who knew Thorin before he became part of our family. People usually commented on how good Thorin looked or how glad they were he was with us. We never experienced hostility in these encounters, but it was always disconcerting. What did they know about Thorin we didn't?

Another type of encounter—more like an intrusion—we continue to experience to this day is strangers who can't get over the fact Thorin has Down syndrome. We found traveling with Thorin must be similar to being with a celebrity. Thorin is recognized by his Down syndrome in the same way Brad Pitt is recognized by his distinctive features. And the same way Mr. Pitt is just as likely to be lionized as condemned, Thorin is also the recipient of a continuum of opinions. In both cases, public people think they know you, and you must engage with them simply because they recognize you.

The first time it happened, I was at Target with Thorin. A woman inexplicably yelled, "I love the way Down syndrome babies look!" I ignored her. Her teenaged daughter looked like she wanted to dig a hole so she could disappear. The woman must have thought I couldn't hear her so she yelled it a couple more times, running along our cart as I sprinted away.

I yelled in her direction before losing her in the housewares department and said, "Okay, that's enough!"

Ward and I started comparing notes on our bizarre stranger stories. We both had encounters with the overly familiar fan who is completely tone-deaf to the concept of stranger danger. Over the years, untold strangers have asked Thorin to hug them. I'm guessing in their mind they think, *I'm not some creepy adult. I just want to hug a boy with Down syndrome.* Early on, Thorin would try to comply with their requests, but either Ward or I would intervene. Later, as Thorin developed a healthier concept of strangers, he would run to me. Insistence is a big feature of this type of intruder. I had one woman repeatedly insist.

"Please, please can he hug me?"

"He really can't," I said putting my arm around Thorin as we walked away.

"How about a high-five then?" she yelled.

Money givers are another fan who Ward has run into on several occasions. This person, without exception, is an elderly woman who presses a dollar bill in Ward's hand and says, "For the boy."

———

In preparing for Thorin's third birthday—his first with us—I wanted to make sure everything was to his liking. I consulted him on the kind of cake, frosting, and decorations by showing him online photos. He wanted a chocolate cake with chocolate frosting, topped with dinosaurs, which I liberally interpreted as anything prehistoric. Ward's mother and brother came from New Jersey for the event. The Burdins and McGirrs from next door came with their girls. And, Jade came.

Jade attended to Thorin's every need and criticized almost everything I did. Her honeymoon period with Ward and me had clearly worn off, and she choose me as the target—similar to Thorin. She liked me and was happy Thorin was with us, but she treated me like the inept stepmother she would have to school in the ways of parenting, which made sense to me since she had sacrificed so much to care for him.

"The wooly mammoth's tusks are too sharp," she said, pointing at the cake.

"I think it'll be fine."

"I'm going to put it up, just in case," she said removing the miniature beast.

I hoped she wouldn't notice the little caveman's spear—placing a third of the decorations in quarantine. In spite of my perceived safety deficits, Thorin had a great birthday. I wasn't convinced Thorin knew what the celebration was for, though. I didn't attribute that to Down syndrome but to the fact this was his third birthday in as many homes. Jade had been at his first birthday but not his second. At this birthday, there were people he had just met, and Sherry was not present. How could he grasp the concept that birthdays are celebrations where the people who love you most get together to celebrate your birth?

We saw Jade at least once a month. She was always on guard for some inadequacy on my part and even signs of mistreatment. A few weeks after his party, we had a visit lined up with her. Thorin had been playing outside, and Ward called him in to change from his muddy clothes. Standing in the kitchen, Thorin lost his footing as he pulled off his jacket. He faced planted on the kitchen floor. I ran to him when I heard him scream. Ward was calmly assessing Thorin's injury while Thorin screamed and sobbed. I, on the other hand, screamed bloody murder upon seeing Thorin's face covered in dripping blood. Thorin took this as his cue to start screaming louder.

"Kari, stop it! It's not that bad," Ward counseled me.

"Not that bad! He's covered in blood!"

Thorin wailed.

"Kari, go in the other room. You're scaring him."

Holy, crap! I was scaring him!

I sat in the living room while Ward updated me.

"He split his lip," he shouted. "It looks fine, almost done bleeding."

"All that blood from a spilt lip?" I shouted back.

"I take it you haven't seen much boxing," he said dryly.

Next, I became terrified at the thought of seeing Jade later that day. I was convinced she would call DHHS.

"Kari, she's not going to do that. You're overreacting," Ward assured me.

"What if I'm not overreacting?"

"I'm going to assume you are, Screamy," he said smirking.

When we saw her, I didn't even have a chance to explain his swollen, bruised lip.

"How exactly did that happen?" she said, touching Thorin's face.

I made the mistake of telling the story to her in a rushed, slightly manic and apologetic way.

"Don't apologize to me; I'm not the one you scarred for life. And screaming? How stupid was that?"

"Well, he looks a million times better now," I said smiling. Privately I thought, *What a ball buster.*

"Except for the fact he needs a haircut," she snapped. I had to hand it to her; she was quick with a comeback.

"Oh, he wants to grow it out," I said, realizing our roles were totally reversed. It was a real *Freaky Friday* situation with Jade. She was the adult.

Jade snorted. "He's three; he doesn't know what he wants. You want to grow it out. Bad idea."

During that same visit, Jade told us Halloween was her favorite holiday so it would probably be Thorin's. Sherry had shared with me that Thorin dressed up as a giraffe the previous year, but he hadn't been trick-or-treating yet.

Later that month, I took Thorin shopping for a costume and offered a number of characters to choose from. He shook his head no at all of them. After ten minutes of trying to figure it out with him, I decided to pick one for him. There was a bee costume that would be toasty warm for trick and treating with Ella and Evvy; it is the only costume I ever picked out for him. From then on, Thorin would plan months in advance for his costume choice, usually an Avenger character. He wears the costume for weeks before Halloween and weeks after. Jade was correct: Halloween is Thorin's favorite holiday, surpassing even Christmas and his bedroom motif.

Five years after that first Halloween together, Thorin and I were sitting in the backyard. It was July. He turned and faced me.

"Thanks you for bee costume."

"The one from when you were little?"

"Yes."

"Wow. You had to wait a long time to be able to tell me that."

"Long time."

"You're welcome. I'm glad I got it right."

⸻

As the weather got colder, Thorin started getting sick. He would get horrible colds; snot would run from his nose, and he would have wracking coughs. One night, I was awakened by what sounded like a seal barking. Thorin was standing in his crib barking and sobbing. I reached to pick him up.

He screamed, "No, Daddy!"

I yelled to Ward who was able to hold Thorin and provide some comfort. I knew it was croup because I had seen *Terms of Endearment.* I suggested, as Debra Winger had demonstrated in the film, we start a hot shower and close the bathroom door with the three of us huddled in the steam. What I discovered is—in that the same way Jack Nicholson would never really be interested in a woman the age of Shirley MacLaine—the steam room treatment was not an actual remedy. Thorin now was not only barking and crying, but he was also screaming and flaying his arms. The three of us had our hair plastered on our head, and we were drenched in sweat.

"He's not better," I said quietly.

Ward mouthed the words, "I'm scared."

Trying not to act as panicked as I felt, I said, "Hey, let's get in the car and go to a place where they help kids who get sick in the middle of the night."

"You think this is bad enough for a hospital!" Ward exclaimed.

I couldn't exactly send Ward to the living room, like he did with me, so I tried to calm Thorin.

"It's not that bad, Sweetie, but we are new at this so we should go to the hospital."

Once there, he surprisingly sounded better. The emergency room doctor verified it was croup. He also told us the reason Thorin improved was that the cold air on way to the hospital probably opened his airways. He told us when it happened again, which it would, to take him for a drive with the windows open. We were shaken but relieved there was an easy fix.

The doctor was right. A couple weeks later, we were awakened by Thorin's barking cough. Again, Thorin only wanted Ward to hold him. Thorin protested going in the car, sobbing. The temperature gauge on the car read 25 degrees as we drove around our neighborhood with the windows down. After twenty minutes, the barking subsided. We got back into bed. Ninety minutes later he was back up barking, so we got in the car for a second tour. Once he quieted down, we went back home. Thorin wouldn't go back to sleep.

"I have to sleep, otherwise I'm a wreck all day," Ward told me.

"Please do then because I find lack of sleep invigorating!"

"Are you being sarcastic? Because that seems unnecessary."

"It's completely necessary, Sleeping Beauty!"

Ward went off to bed. I lay with Thorin on the couch and watched old Barney Miller episodes. While Coco slept upstairs, likely in Ward's arms, Walt climbed onto the couch lying down with his head upright, inches from Thorin. Thorin and I fell asleep. Every so often, I would rouse myself to check on Thorin. I found Walt was still on guard, watchful and alert. After that night, Walt stopped sleeping on our bed and moved into Thorin's room to sleep curled up on the rug next to his crib.

In the morning, I called Sherry.

"Yeah, he was sick all last winter. So awful sick with the croup. It was scary. I worried about his health."

His primary doctor reassured us that it was common for someone with a compromised immune system and Down syndrome to be sick often. During that winter, there were three more trips to the emergency room when driving around the neighborhood with the windows down was not enough. On one of those visits, Thorin was admitted. Something different happened that night; the barking became a tight high-pitched sound as he inhaled. He looked like he was struggling with his breathing. His eyes were opened wide.

When we got to the hospital, they immediately gave Thorin oxygen. His chest heaved, and he beat his fists at his side. I felt wild inside. Ward and I stood against the wall in silence as we watched the doctor and nurse help Thorin. When he calmed down, the doctor turned to us.

"Don't worry, it's just stridor."

"It seemed like he struggled breathing though," I told him, my voice tight.

"Oh, I'm sure he did. Stridor feels like you are breathing through a straw."

The three of us stayed in the hospital room together: Thorin slept in an over-sized crib, and Ward and I slept together on a single bed. Strangely, it was one of the most peaceful nights of sleep any of us had in weeks. Thorin was well attended to, so Ward and I knew we wouldn't be woken in the middle of the night to Thorin's screams, rousing us for a drive to the hospital—we were already there.

Thorin was given a nebulizing treatment, antibiotics, and steroids. We were told to get a cool mist vaporizer for his room, and if he showed the slightest sign of being sick, we should keep him home from school. One emergency room doctor told us that once the warm weather was back Thorin would be good again. I didn't take much comfort in that since winter in Maine is about six months long.

Thorin's illness was frightening for him, of course, and us. It also caused Thorin stress; he missed school, and his development was interrupted. It stressed my relationship with Ward, and I felt lonely. I was lucky to have my sister, Betty, who listened to my fears, cleaned our apartment, did laundry, and made meals for us.

During this time, Ward and I both read books, articles, and blog posts on Down syndrome, first looking for information on health concerns, particularly respiratory ones. We learned children with Down syndrome have smaller and narrower nasal passages and airways. As a result, they are more prone to croup and stridor. Aside from the medical information we found, Ward and I were struck again by the repetitive narrative by both medical professionals and parents on the issue of grief. A common experience described by parents was finding out they were going to have a baby with Down syndrome or the baby was delivered and had Down syndrome. The parents would then reassure the reader that ultimately they accepted their child with Down syndrome.

It isn't that I couldn't understand how someone might feel that way, but I couldn't relate at all. It was love at first sight followed by months of fear at the thought of losing Thorin. I believed the grief of actually losing him would have broken me.

"I think there's another story that needs to be out there," I told Ward.

"I've been thinking the same thing. I'd like to tackle the atypical piece, too. That division can really suck if you're the atypical one."

In the course of a sentence, we went from discussing the dominant storyline in what we were reading to the life we were living and wanted to share.

"Could we do a blog?" I asked.

"Yeah. We're good writers. We have something interesting to say. That's enough."

We knew we couldn't do anything until after the adoption. Thorin was still legally a ward of the state. We couldn't post photos of him on Facebook or allow photo releases at his school and we certainly couldn't write about him on a blog. For the months leading up to his adoption, we researched how to set up a blog and discussed what it was we thought we had to offer.

"I want this to be about Thorin, not us," I said.

"I get it."

"Right. And, Thorin may want to read this someday so . . ."

"Let's be careful about what we write and focus on what he would want to share."

"Yes!" I enthusiastically agreed.

"Okay, he's our protagonist. It should be named after him."

"Right. And, it should be funny whenever possible," I suggested.

"He's a funny kid."

We batted blog names and ideas back and forth for months.

"What about *Thunder Boy*? Thorin means Thunder!" Ward offered.

"Love it!"

Even though we would eventually discard *Thunder Boy* as a possibility, Thorin later became obsessed with the Avengers, particularly Thor, the god of the thunder.

A few weeks later, we considered *Extraordinary Boy* but agreed it was showy. Then one afternoon, Ward called sounding excited.

"I got it!"

"Lay it on me!"

"*A Typical Boy*! It works both ways, the way the world sees him—separate, apart—and the way we see him—like any kid. Bonus, it's a Warren Zevon song!"

"I love it! You're brilliant!"

We then found out it was taken as a blog name, proving someone else's brilliance. So we tweaked the name and settled happily on *A Typical Son*.

"I think we should have a quote on the blog that unifies our intention. I think it should be . . ."

"Whitman!" we spoke in unison.

We started scouring *Leaves of Grass* for the quote that would define our philosophy. One night in bed, Ward passed me the book opened to "Song of Myself." He ran his finger over the text he wanted me to read: ". . . I exist as I am, that is enough."

"Yeah, Baby! That's true for everyone!" I cheered.

"Exactly," Ward said as he turned off the light.

———

I did believe in "that is enough," but there were times it was tested. Thorin was three and a half years old. He was sitting on the coffee table in the living room, looking at a Curious George book.

"Where go?" he asked as I walked through the room.

"I'm going to the bathroom."

"I'm going to read book."

I stopped dead in my tracks.

"Ward, did you hear that!" I yelled.

Ward ran into the room, "I did! Buddy, that was fantastic!"

"Thorin you said a complete sentence!"

"No!" shouted Thorin.

I thought maybe some communication miracle had happened. I hoped Thorin was free to express himself. As days passed without that kind of communication happening again, I first felt disappointment then I meditated on Whitman. I was thrilled about Thorin's sentence because it was how I communicated. I valued it more and certainly not as "enough." There is no lesser or greater communication; there is only "communication." I made the mistake of sharing Thorin's sentence with the speech therapist.

"Have you ever heard of that sort of thing? Is it spontaneous speech?"

"No, I have never heard of that."

Of course you never heard of it. Dashed hopes is your forte.

It would be almost four years before Thorin would spontaneously say a complete sentence of that length.

Seven months after Thorin's mother had surrendered her parental rights, we were notified of our adoption date. It would take place the following month. After that we would be parents sans the state of Maine.

When I contacted Linda, she asked if the caseworker who had physically removed Thorin from his home over two years before could come to the proceedings. She explained the woman had been hoping the best for Thorin since then and wanted to see him on the big day. A few other staff members who had interaction with Thorin also asked to be included. I realized how much of an impact not only Thorin but also all the children in the system had on the professionals who mostly saw the anguish of their young charges and not the celebrations. Aside from DHHS staff, family members, friends, Karen, Jade, and Jade's foster parents attended. Twenty people squeezed into the judge's chambers.

Thorin was wearing the outfit I purchased a few days before: a white oxford shirt, a striped tie, a navy blazer, grey slacks, and black dress shoes. I wore a charcoal skirt with a white linen blouse, and

Ward wore gray slacks, a white shirt, a tie, and a navy blazer. We looked dapper and ready to graduate to being a fully legal family.

The judge's role was brief, mainly reading legal texts and asking for signatures. He did ask if anyone wanted to say anything. I looked at Ward holding Thorin. Thorin had a wide smile on his face. Ward and I had already decided I would say something on our behalf.

As I looked at everyone who brought us to this moment and those who were sharing in our rite of passage, I could feel the lump in my throat before I started speaking. I blinked away my tears and nodded to indicate I was ready to start.

"Ward and I want to thank Thorin's parents for creating him; Jade for saving him; Sherry for caring for him; Linda for knowing he was for us; and Thorin for making us the luckiest parents in the world."

***

The day we adopted Thorin, we launched the blog *a typical son*: April 1, 2010. My opening post explained why we chose the name *a typical son*, and I related our first IEP meeting. From then on, Ward and I traded back and forth between posts. The early posts were a non-linear telling of the ways of state adoptions and our experience as new parents. Our readership was mainly family and friends.

One of Ward's high school classmates left a comment that expressed the sentiment we hoped to convey: "I used to feel bad for people like you. I thought it must be so awful. Now I'm ashamed, you are like me."

Adoption Day

CHAPTER FOUR

How I Earned the Privilege of Being Called Mommy

Thorin's health did improve when the weather changed, but not as dramatically as we would have liked. I thought we should be more proactive, so I found a pediatrician who had several children with Down syndrome as patients. She was a doctor of osteopathy (DO). Her focus was on using osteopathic manipulation to stimulate a child's immune system. It seemed perfect for Thorin.

During one of his sick visits, I asked his pediatrician for a referral. First he snorted, which I took to mean he didn't respect DOs. Second he said, "If he were normal, I'd say no. But because nothing can help him, I will grant that request."

Did he just fucking say that? I didn't know how to respond. I turned to Thorin, and he reached inside his diaper then brought his hand back out and wiggled his fingers, all the while staring at the doctor. *Good grief, Thorin did have balls!* I hadn't seen that kind of male domination since Joe Pesci in *Goodfellas.*

The doctor's face turned blotchy red. He told me to pick up the referral from the receptionist then he left the room.

"He's a jerk," I muttered in disgust.

Thorin nodded yes.

We had countless appointments with other specialists for various conditions and symptoms: a nutritionist, a geneticist, an eye doctor, a urologist, and the worst dentist, ever. Thorin had come to us with bad teeth. He had three root canals, and two of his teeth had been capped in silver while with Sherry. His front two teeth were deteriorating. I took him for a cleaning, and the hygienist went at his teeth manically. Thorin was lying on his back with his eyes shut tightly.

"Can you be more gentle, please. Those teeth are so fragile."

"I have to do this."

I laughed at the absurdity of her answer.

"You don't have to do it that hard."

After she finished, the dentist came in, examined Thorin's teeth, and sent us home. The next morning, Thorin walked into the kitchen, smiling at me. I saw both front teeth had broken off during the night. All that remained were little jagged stubs. I silently congratulated myself on not screaming. Ward and I were both concerned he could cut the inside of his mouth, so I called the answering service for the dentist.

"That happened sooner than we thought," the dentist said when he called back.

I ignored his blasé attitude.

"Okay, but it's still concerning even if it was anticipated by you."

"What do you want me to do, it's Saturday?"

"I want you to meet us at your office this morning."

I heard an exaggerated sigh from the dentist.

"I'll see you in forty-five minutes."

At the clinic, he assured us Thorin would not cut his mouth. Then, I followed up on the comment he made during our phone call.

"If you knew this was going to happen, why didn't you recommend pulling the teeth yesterday?"

"Pulling teeth can be traumatizing for a three-year-old," he said authoritatively.

How could he possibly think having Thorin's teeth break off during the night would be less traumatizing? There was no further discussion or apology; the dentist quickly scheduled an appointment for that Monday to pull what remained of Thorin's teeth and sent us home.

Before we went back to the dentist, two days later, I told Thorin, "We're going to the dentist. He'll give you a shot that might sting for a second. It will make your mouth numb so it won't hurt when he pulls out your teeth. We can go to Target after, and you can pick out a toy."

Thorin nodded. I asked if he had questions. He shook his head no. This procedure must have seemed like small potatoes to him after having dental surgery in the hospital.

When we walked into the small bay, the dentist was waiting. Thorin pointed to the screen on the ceiling above the examination chair and said "on" as he signed "please." The hygienist had him make a selection. He chose SpongeBob and settled in the chair to watch. I proudly told the doctor how I prepared Thorin for the procedure.

"You told him I was going to hurt him?" He sounded wounded.

"No. I said the shot might sting," in an upbeat way.

"Why, why? Now he's going to hate me!"

That seemed like a dramatic response, even to me. Thorin looked up for a second and went back to SpongeBob.

"Oh, he won't hate you," I said reassuringly. "So the shot won't sting?" I said, asking for clarification.

"Stop saying that!"

Thorin looked up at me. I shrugged my shoulders. It took everything not to cross my eyes.

"Okay, sorry, maybe we should just get going," I said soothingly.

"I'm the dentist! I say when!" By now, he sounded a little hysterical.

I wanted to say, "Good grief, man, pull it together!" But I feared I would make him cry. When he was ready, he turned to Thorin and began.

"I'm putting some magic sauce on your gums."

Thorin looked at me with a wrinkled brow. As he injected the shot of Novocain, Thorin did buck a little in the chair.

The dentist shot me a dirty look. "That's your doing!"

After he pulled the second tooth, Thorin sat up, made the sign for "done," and started to get out of the chair.

"I'll tell you when to get out the chair, young man," admonished the dentist.

The dentist soon left, and the hygienist cleaned up Thorin. We left and, as promised, headed to Target. In the car, I told Thorin he looked like a really cool vampire, which made him happy.

When Ward got home that evening, I told him we needed a new dentist.

"Okay, so we're up to three professionals you want to axe, is that right? The doctor, maybe the speech therapist, and now the dentist."

"I think that's right."

"How about the dentist first and wait on the others? People say ignorant things. I agree we can't overlook the whole broken teeth, high-strung dentist situation."

"The other two are on thin ice, though."

"Fine," he said patting my shoulder.

———

Parenting is about discovery. I discovered I loved picking out clothes for Thorin. I loved putting together outfits for him that made a statement. I knew this was going to be a short-term passion, and Thorin would develop his own style at some point.

I realized I was obsessed with his look the day I dressed him in blue jeans, a yellow, cotton, long-sleeve shirt untucked under a blue vest that had black, blue, and mustard stripes across the chest. The look that day was 1966 British schoolboy. Thorin's hair was long and shaggy, very Brian Jones, the original founder of The Rolling Stones. When I picked him up from school, his yellow shirt was tucked in. *How had that happened?* Whoever tucked in his shirt had no sense of style.

Once we got in the car, I asked, "Thorin, who tucked in your shirt?

Thorin shook his head no.

"Is that hard to explain to me?"

"Yesith."

"Thorin, this is very important. If anyone tries to tuck in your shirt next time you wear this outfit, I want you to untuck it. Be polite but make it clear you want it out. Okay?"

He gave me a thumbs-up. The next time I dressed him in that outfit, he stood up and pulled hard on the bottom of the shirt, smiling.

I even had fans of my stylist abilities. I ran into a friend who told me her daughter was interning at a preschool. The daughter was taken with a little boy there who wore great outfits. In fact, she had a nickname for him: College Boy.

"It's Thorin!" I yelled.

She laughed, "It is Thorin!"

Ward would often offer to dress Thorin. I couldn't risk having him put together an outfit I would find unsuitable but I didn't want to be insulting about it.

"Oh, thank you. I already laid clothes out if you want to use those!"

It took months before Ward caught on.

"It's almost like you don't trust me to dress him."

Laughing, I said, "Well that's a weird thing to think."

———

Thorin's aide at school was named Mindy. She looked to be in her early forties. Her personality was exuberant with a touch of manic. She stood five-feet tall, had washboard abs, ropy arms like Madonna, and shiny, straight hair. I felt like a big clod next to her. At the end of the first day with Thorin, she told me she loved him. It was clearly level jumping but it was also clear he felt the same way about her.

Mindy became devoted to Thorin. She took time to quiz his physical therapist, occupational therapist, and speech therapist about what more she could do to help him. I found out from Mindy that she worked a second job, was raising a teenager, and helped raise her grandchild. Yet in her spare time, which must have been while she was going to the bathroom, she taught herself some signing to better communicate with Thorin.

Her only shortcoming seemed to be that she went a little overboard sometimes. When I would pick up Thorin at the end of the day, she would fawn over him, hugging and kissing him.

"I love you, Thorin! I love you so much! I'll miss you!"

I wanted to shout, "Sweet Jesus, Mindy, stop!"

I didn't want to risk alienating her, but her routine was making it difficult to get Thorin to leave with me. After a week of it, I took her aside.

"Listen, Mindy, my job is to drop off Thorin and act like it's no biggie. Your job is to do the same at the end of the day. No biggie. Do you understand?"

"I just really love him!" she said.

"Mindy, I get that. He loves you, too, but you're acting like you're sending him off to war. The thing is, Mindy, you're sending him home with me—his mother."

"Oh, no! I'm so sorry!" She looked like she was going to cry.

"Mindy, I'm sorry. I didn't mean to . . ." I trailed off.

I had a complicated relationship with Mindy. Thorin was still not calling me Mom, and he was clearly in love with her. I was jealous of Mindy. I had to remind myself we were lucky to have her. I also knew that if Thorin were on a field trip, singing to the elderly at a nursing home and a grizzly bear broke into the building, Mindy would kick his ass seven ways to Sunday before he got to Thorin.

———

Thorin's preschool used a model of childcare that accentuated the positive. They believed so strongly in their methodology that they proselytized their message daily. For example, I was encouraged to say, "Use your quiet feet" instead of "Stop running!" I would never say to anyone, "Use your quiet feet," so why would I talk to Thorin like that? It was also recommended I ignore it when Thorin threw things. I didn't think the teacher knew what we were up against at home.

"You know that scene in the movie *Carrie*," I began telling her, "when she makes all that cutlery fly around the kitchen? That's every room in our house—except replace the cutlery with toy cars, shoes, cups, dishes, eyeglasses, remote controls, books, and almost a mini-dachshund."

She gave me a sympathetic smile. "That's because you aren't ignoring it."

Of course she would say that. Then I wondered, *What is the positive directive of "Don't throw Coco?"*

I thought the preschool's intentions were good but I didn't want to hear what I should be doing. I was Thorin's mother even if he didn't acknowledge it.

———

As the weather changed, so did Thorin's health. The middle of the night trips around the neighborhood in the car and visits to the emergency room began once more. Seeing Thorin helpless was punishing. Dr. Not-McDreamy, as I came to refer to his pediatrician privately, prescribed a nebulizer to use at home.

As he gave me the compact machine and a box of ampules filled with albuterol, I asked, "Maybe he has asthma?"

"He doesn't," he said authoritatively.

A couple weeks after I brought home the nebulizer, Thorin woke us in the middle of the night. He was making the dreaded stridor sound. As I ran to his crib, I had the mental image of him trying to breathe through a straw.

"I'll set up the nebulizer," I told Ward.

Ward lifted him from the crib and carried him into our room. Walt followed them to our bed, curling up against Thorin as he lay propped up on the pillows. I went to put the little mask over Thorin's face. He pushed my hands away. He was still making the shrieking sound then he started gasping for air. I saw the panic in Thorin's eyes. Ward picked him up and starting pacing. Thorin's back was arching. He started banging his head with his fists. Then he was clawing at his throat.

"We have to call an ambulance," I said as calmly as possible.

"No, it can't be that bad," said Ward. "Maybe we should wait."

I grabbed my phone and called 911. The dispatcher answered.

"I don't know if our son can breathe." I could hear my voice breaking and felt my heart pounding in my ears.

With her assistance, I was able to give her all the information to send help. The three of us went to sit on the front steps. The hospital was less than a five-minute drive from our apartment. We focused on keeping Thorin calm, talking in soothing tones. Ward gently held his thrashing body.

I hoped the cold outside would open his airways. When I saw no change, I started silently pleading to God. Once the ambulance arrived, the paramedics moved quickly. They brought oxygen to the porch.

"Shouldn't he go in there?" I said pointing to the ambulance.

They gave a quick look to each other. "We need to do as much as we can here," one of the paramedics said.

In my head, I just kept saying please over and over again. One paramedic went to the ambulance to make a call to the hospital. The other one tried giving oxygen to Thorin, but he was fighting him, shaking his head and pushing away the paramedic's hands.

"Hey, Dad, you gotta hold him still!" he said to Ward.

When the other guy came back, he was still talking to the hospital. In conferring with the person on the other end of the line, it was decided they give Thorin a shot.

Suddenly, I was looking down on the scene from above. I could see Thorin struggling; Ward and I stricken with fear; the paramedics busy with the details of administering aid; and the ambulance with flashing lights. Just as suddenly, I was jerked back in my body.

It was clear the paramedics were looking for a specific response from Thorin. When it didn't come, and after conferring again with the hospital, one paramedic told us it was time to move. Ward, carrying Thorin, jumped into the back of the ambulance with the guy on the phone. I got in the front seat with the driver. He didn't look at me. He also didn't say anything to me, such as "It's going to be fine" or "Don't worry." So, I asked.

"Is he going to be okay?"

"How old is he?"

I looked at the driver's profile. His arms were rigid, and his hands grasped the wheel tightly. He drove very fast. When we came to a one-way street, he pulled on to the street instead of bypassing it.

"We don't want to waste time," the driver said as we sped down the street.

If we'd gone the other way it would have been another three blocks, too many in his mind. I gave up hope Thorin would be okay.

I checked out again—not as an observer above the scene but completely gone. The next thing I remembered was being on a stretcher with Thorin lying on top of me. His chest was against mine. I could feel his breathing was still labored, but his chest wasn't heaving wildly. He was crying quietly. He reached up and put his hand on my neck, slick with tears. I looked up and saw we were in a room with several people in white coats. A doctor had her hand on Thorin's back; she stroked his hair. He pulled closer to me.

"He's okay, gentlemen," she said to the paramedics. "He's going to be okay."

"He made a liar of me," the driver said. "He was coding out! He was!"

She looked up at him, "Yes, he was. He turned it around though."

Even in that moment, I thought it was interesting that she gave credit to Thorin.

"Okay, most of you can leave. We have it under control, thankfully," she said.

A nurse lifted Thorin while I moved from the stretcher. Another nurse put tubes in his nose for oxygen, then she hooked him up to a monitor. Thorin did not fight her. After several minutes, Thorin fell asleep. Ward and I sat next to his bed, holding hands.

"Did I pass out? Is that why I was on the stretcher?" I asked Ward.

Ward laughed softly, "What?"

"I checked out. I don't remember everything."

"You seemed like you were there. When we got out of the ambulance, Thorin reached for you. They told you to get on the stretcher so you could hold him."

The staff moved the three of us to a hospital room for the night. Thorin refused to sleep in the oversize crib so we squished together in the single-sized hospital bed. Ward and I turned inward toward Thorin while he slept on his back in the middle. I don't know if I slept so much as my state of consciousness took a break from what could have been.

I was the first one awake. I opened my eyes. I was still facing Thorin and didn't want to move. My chest and upper arms were aching from clenching my body the night before. I looked at Ward and Thorin, relieved we made it through the worst of it. Thorin opened his eyes. He turned his body toward mine. He had an impish grin on his face.

"Hi, Mommy," he said as he put both hands on either side of my face.

He said it! I had finally proved my mettle. I also knew him well enough to know if I made mention of it he might never call me that again.

"Good morning, Sweetheart," I said. "How are you?"

"Good, Mom," he replied. He never again called me Ba.

———

After we got home, I called Dr. Not-McDreamy for a referral to a pulmonologist. His nurse called back to tell me he thought my request was completely unnecessary.

"Will he take responsibility for another emergency room visit?" I asked.

When she called back twenty-five minutes later, she said he would like to make a referral to a pediatric pulmonologist.

A week later, I sat in the reception area of the pulmonology clinic with Thorin, filling out questions on the intake forms.

- How many days of school has your child missed in the last six months?
- Does your child awake during the night coughing?
- Does your child awake during the night having difficulty breathing?
- How many trips to the emergency room in the last six months?
- How many times did you call an ambulance in the last six months?

My immediate thought was the doctor was assessing our competency as parents. As the questions continued, I noodled out they were assessing Thorin's pulmonary health; all were common markers that children with asthma shared. We weren't awful parents; however, we put too much trust in someone we didn't respect. The pulmonologist was easy going and personable. Instead of facing a computer screen, he faced us as he wrote on a yellow legal pad, looking up as I spoke. After I described the night we called an ambulance, he nodded and said, "You made the right decision; those situations can go bad quickly."

A breathing test was done to confirm what the doctor already suspected: Thorin had asthma. He prescribed a daily maintenance inhaler, a rescue inhaler, plus the continued use of the nebulizer as needed. He also gave us a protocol explaining what symptoms indicated the need for more than a daily inhaler. He said to get rid of the cool air vaporizer, explaining wet air was about the worst thing for asthma.

"Why did our doctor and the hospital recommend it?" I asked.

"Because they aren't pulmonologists," he replied.

Then, the pulmonologist recommended we make an appointment to see a pediatrician he worked with regularly. She also happened to be a DO.

The new pediatrician was the complete opposite of Dr. Not-McDreamy. When she entered the exam room, she turned toward Thorin with her hand out and said, "Hello, Thorin! I'm Dr. Peggy." After they shook hands, she turned her attention to me. The entire tone of the exam was positive toward Thorin. She mostly asked yes or no questions, starting with Thorin for an answer and then asking me for more detail. It was clear she assumed Thorin was competent and could participate. Toward the end of the exam, she asked if we could talk privately. We went to another exam room.

Holy crap, she's going to tell me something awful.

I must have looked alarmed. She laughed and put her arm on mine.

"He's okay. He's great! I wanted to tell you that I know Thorin."

It took me a second to understand.

"From before?" I asked.

"Yeah, from before. I was a resident at the hospital when he was brought in. I was part of his care team. He was so sick. He was a fighter. Everyone fell in love with him. When we found out he was going back home, we were worried. I didn't know what happened after that. Then when I saw his name on my schedule . . . I was so happy! I was so relieved! I never stopped thinking about Thorin."

"You're supposed to be his doctor!"

"I know!"

Thorin's health started improving. He still got sick frequently but not in such a debilitating way. He was in school more frequently, bouncing back more quickly. It was then I actually became a bit of a hypervigilant parent. I was so used to taking him to the ER that I started worrying I was being lax. The school called one day telling me he was sick and sobbing. When I got there, someone mentioned his breathing being ragged.

"Ragged? What's ragged mean to you?" I demanded.

"Not quite right? I don't know exactly," she said nervously.

I watched her intently and said, "Do you think he may have trouble breathing?"

"I guess he could have a hard time breathing." Her response was measured.

That was all I needed to hear. Later, I realized I frightened her. What childcare provider wants to find out a child in her care should have gone to the hospital?

I practically threw Thorin in the car and drove to the ER. He and I walked in together, which should have been a sign he did not need to be there—I wasn't carrying him in.

"I think my son is having a problem breathing," I said in a shaky voice at the admitting desk.

The woman looked at me askance—maybe the most askance I've ever been looked at. "You mean that boy?" she said pointing behind me.

I turned and saw Thorin dancing up a storm, taking full advantage of the shiny floor in the entryway.

"Gee, he looks better," I said. "Maybe I overreacted."

"What do you want to do, Mom?" she asked.

"I guess we'll just go, then."

I slunk out with Thorin twirling behind me. I was mortified. As I explained it to Ward later, he suggested this insight: "You can freak out now. You couldn't then. It had to come out some place. And now you know if he's dancing, he's okay."

When I was merely a hypothetical parent, my theoretical child behaved as I instructed him. I was convinced my deeply satisfying fantasy world as a parent was possible. As a non-parent, I would listen to my friends complain about how hard it was to get their children to go to sleep or stay in their own bed. In my mind, I would judge them for not being able to control their children through the same calm reasoning I had great success with in my imagination.

Once I became an actual parent, I quickly realized that until you have actually struggled to get a toddler to bed, you couldn't truly understand how devious yet universally predictable toddlers are. How on earth did Thorin know to ask for water, take a sip, and then twenty minutes later say he had to go to the bathroom?

One particular night, Thorin and I were lying on our sides in bed, facing each other. "Going to sleep" had started forty minutes earlier. I had cheerfully read countless children's books and knew I couldn't summon the enthusiasm necessary to read about a freaking fuzzy duckling. Instead, I started reading aloud the *New Yorker* article on Scientology. My mom told me I loved it when my dad used to sing the sports page to me. Thorin kept saying no to the indictments against L. Ron Hubbard, which began to sound like a bleating lamb.

"How 'bout if I sing it to you?"

"No!"

It was then I stumbled upon an idea.

"Do you want to know how we met?" I asked.

My question was met with enthusiasm. "Yesith!"

"Okay! Good! Here's how it happened. Mommy and Daddy wanted a little boy. One day, we got a phone call from a lady named Linda who said she knew this two-year-old boy who was really great and wanted a family."

"Me!" he said.

"That's right! It was you! We told Linda we wanted you to be our son. After that, we thought about you all the time. Soon, you became the only thing we thought about."

Thorin clapped excitedly.

I asked, "You wondered how we met?"

Nodding his head and laughing he said, "Yesith!"

I had a stab of guilt. Of course any child would wonder how he became part of his family, but most children could ask.

"I should've told you before. Okay, so one day, Linda sent me a photo of you. You were so beautiful I cried. Daddy cried, too. I kept your picture in my purse. I would look at it all day. I would talk to you. I would tell you how much I loved you."

Thorin made a sighing sound.

"Then we finally met you! The rest you know."

He jumped up and down on the bed. When he stopped, he signed, "Again."

"You want to hear it again?"

"Yesith!"

The story became a nightly ritual, which Thorin initiated by making the sign for "again" at bedtime. We started calling it the "Again Story." I realized Thorin was in a position where he would have to wait until I asked him a question to figure out what he wanted to know. It made me wonder what else I was missing. I thought the next logical step was asking him if he wanted to know how Ward and I met.

"Me there?" he asked.

"No, just Daddy and me."

"No, tanks."

———

I wasn't just experiencing a learning curve on communicating with Thorin but with many of the women at the school. I loved the school, and, most importantly, Thorin loved the school, but I was becoming exhausted by their continual unsolicited advice. The staff got me through his first field trip, assuring me he would be okay. They were sympathetic to his health needs. They administered his rescue inhaler and, if needed, his nebulizer. They made accommodations. Thorin refused to nap, so one of teachers built a little cardboard house over his sleeping mat, and he could play as long as he was not disturbing the other children. He was absolutely safe there.

I just didn't want to sing "The Goodbye Song" when Thorin didn't want to leave. When I found out there was also a "Clean-up Song," I just shook my head.

Who's writing these crappy propaganda songs? What's wrong with "Listen here, Mister, you made the mess so help me pick this stuff up?"

When I was a child, my parents often used work experiences to give me context for my behavior. Say, I was running through the house screaming, so my dad might tell me, "If you did that at work, it'd be all over with. It's easy to find non-screaming workers." That logic seemed fine to me.

I found out from Ward the staff never said anything to him.

"What? Why don't they tell you what to do?"

"Kari, I'm a man. No one expects us to do anything."

"That sucks!"

"I don't take it personally and I'm relieved not to hear the feedback."

One afternoon when Thorin wouldn't leave school with me, the speech therapist, who didn't have children, responded with, "Okay, Thorin, should we walk out of the school like a monkey or roll like a log?"

Roll like a log? No fucking way!

I was not going to be able to watch my son and an adult roll down two hallways and out of the school without my head exploding.

"Okay, no, thank you, we aren't going to do either one of those."

I looked at Thorin. "Get up and move it if you want a Popsicle at home."

"We find bribery doesn't work," she suggested.

I wanted to scream, "Shut up!"

I decided against telling her tell I had a bag of M&Ms in my purse in anticipation of tantrums in the supermarket. Rather than peel a screaming, spread-eagled Thorin off the floor, I would lean down and whisper, "If you want two M&Ms, get up now!"

I ended up being thankful for that ludicrous exchange with her because it got me to finally talk to Louise, the school director.

"I know you have our family's best interest at heart. I really, absolutely know that. But if I don't ask for advice or a suggestion on how to deal with Thorin, please have your staff refrain from offering it."

"Who did that?"

"All of you!" I responded too harshly. "I mean most of you. Actually you do it, too, Louise."

It was a couple years of resentment coming out at once.

"I do? I'm so sorry!"

"I should have said something before. I'm sorry, too. I still want to ask for your advice. I value it." Then I told her about rolling like a log.

"Oh, no. The monkey isn't bad but . . ." She looked at the expression on my face and continued, "But if you don't want to be a monkey, it's bad."

We both laughed.

"Don't worry about this. I'm going to take care of it!"

And she did. The unsolicited advice stopped.

I thought we were on an even keel at school until one morning I brought Thorin in to find out Mindy had left without putting in any notice. Thorin was beside himself, and my heart went out to him. He really did love her and not being able to say goodbye was difficult. He couldn't articulate it, but what I saw was the pain of abandonment—something Thorin was all too familiar with. He would tear up when he asked about her, which was constantly. I asked Louise if she could contact Mindy to send a note addressed to Thorin at the school. Louise didn't have any luck. Thorin needed closure. I didn't see any other alternative but to send Thorin a card as Mindy. To make my card believable, I mentioned a couple of things I knew they both loved.

> *Dear Thorin,*
> *This is Mindy. I'm sorry I left without saying goodbye. I had a chance to go live with some elephants on an elephant farm and sing songs all day. You know how much I like elephants and singing. I hope you can forgive me for leaving without saying goodbye. I miss you. I love you.*
>
> *Mindy*

Thorin was thrilled to hear from her. She had no longer disappeared from his life; she hadn't abandoned him. He was able to understand she had this irresistible opportunity that prevented her from seeing him.

My family had a relative on my dad's side who went to the "big house" for stealing nurses' purses. That's how my mom would bring it up to my dad when denigrating his side of the family: "Well, your half-brother went away for stealing nurses' purses."

I first noticed Thorin might also have an issue with taking things that weren't his while waiting in an exam room at one of his doctor's appointments. While I sat in a chair reading a magazine, Thorin sat on the floor pulling out the contents of his backpack. He would briefly inspect the object then set it on the floor to pull out something else. I saw diapers, a package of wipes, a Lightning McQueen glove I didn't recognize, some loose Goldfish crackers, a sumo wrestler doll, a light blue marker I had been missing, and a crumpled piece of paper that I picked up and read. It was a note I had missed from one of his teachers at school: "Thorin really likes chicken fingers!"

I might not have given much thought to my marker or a stray glove, but next Thorin pulled out a laminated photo I immediately recognized as one of his classmates. The photo of her was the one that had been affixed to her cubby at school. I leaned down to pick it up.

"Did, you take this from Chloe's cubby?"

Thorin smiled and grabbed it back, putting it in the bag. The next day, I secretly reattached her photo to the cubby because I didn't want the teachers to know Thorin might be a kleptomaniac.

The following week, I found Chloe's picture was stuck to one of Thorin's hats as I pulled it out of his backpack.

"Please stop taking Chloe's photo. I'm the one who will get in trouble, not you."

In response, Thorin pretended to twirl a fake mustache.

Where did he learn that?

At another doctor's appointment, he stuffed a handful of Viagra brochures into his bag while I was reading *People* magazine. I didn't discover his haul until we got home. When I confronted him with them, he pretended he didn't know anything about it. With all these doctors' appointments, I wondered if "nurses' purses" were just around the corner. I didn't bring the brochures back, probably giving false hope to some drug rep.

Thorin would often go to work with me after I picked him up from school. He would get bored in the office and leave to visit Patty, the receptionist for our floor. One morning after Thorin had visited the day before, Patty came into my office to ask if I borrowed the master key from her desk. It was a fair question: I had locked myself out of my office several times and even once with Thorin in it. I told Patty that I didn't have the key.

The key would be hard to miss. It was attached to a six-inch, red and white, wooden bowling pin by two feet of beaded chain. The search for the master key went on for three days. Patty talked to scores of tenants. She was getting pressure from the landlord who would soon have to rekey the locks to all the offices. Patty came back to talk to me a second time. This time she closed the door behind her.

"Listen, I want you to check Thorin's backpack for that key."

"You do?" I said innocently even though her question prompted me to immediately suspect Thorin of the crime.

"Yes, I do. He took that girl's photo and all those Viagra brochures! I just bet he took that key!"

I made a mental note to never tell Patty anything ever again. Why hadn't I considered Thorin was the likely suspect? I could imagine him eyeing the bowling pin thinking how great it would look in his backpack. Patty reminded me twice before I left to look in his bag, as did the landlord. I promised to call either way later that day.

The first thing I did when I got to the school was look in his bag. There I found the master key wrapped in a *Star Wars* T-shirt. I decided to confront him unexpectedly with the evidence. I thought the element of surprise might unnerve him. My opportunity came on the drive home at a red light where we were about thirty car lengths back. I would have sufficient time to interrogate him, and he wouldn't have anywhere to go.

I reached in and pulled out the master key, turning in my seat and giving it my best bad cop tone. "Look familiar to you, Thorin?"

I saw the recognition in his eyes, and then he made the double thumbs-up sign as he kicked his legs excitedly.

"Thorin, you got your friend Patty in trouble!"

That only elicited belly laughing. When he finally stopped, he gave a contented sigh as he turned to stare out the window the rest of the ride.

After we got home and Thorin was in the other room, I put the master key on a table out of his reach and line of vision. The next morning it was gone! *How did he know where it was? Had he read my mind? Crap!* I had already called the office to say I would return it.

I looked in his backpack, aka his booty bag, but it wasn't there. *Where did Baby Face Nelson put it?* It was useless to ask him. I knew I couldn't break him. I had to think like him.

Okay, I'm a criminal and I am on the short side. Where would I put a valued possession?

After a thorough search, I found the bowling pin under the sink in his play kitchen. I knew he was on to me. I didn't say a word to him.

Ward and I decided to stay on top of his questionable tendencies by calmly addressing the occurrences as they happened but not make a big deal out of it. We saw it as a phase. I wrote about Thorin's kleptomania and the master key incident on the blog. I thought it was a great example of how typical Thorin could be developmentally. We decided not all the examples of Thorin should be shining examples of human behavior. We weren't interested in creating an emblematic personality but relating Thorin's complexity as a human being through real life stories. It also belied the stereotype that children with Down syndrome weren't capable of guile. Ward and I found Thorin could be as cunning as any child.

Soon after I posted the kleptomania story, Ward heard from one of his relatives who shared, "You should be concerned; Kari thinks this kind of thing is funny." Everybody's a critic.

***

Something that was truly not funny was how often Ward and I argued. The glow of parenting had been replaced with the stale plot lines of any sitcom where the husband and wife quarrel about division of labor. Except in our case, unfortunately, it was more of a melodrama. I was so desperate I even bought *What Shamu Taught Me about Life, Love, and Marriage: Lessons for People from Animals and Their Trainers.* The author used animal training strategies to get her husband to pick up his clothes and stop bothering her while she was cooking. It fell apart for me almost immediately because I forgot how much I objected to places like SeaWorld, plus her strategies reminded me of the "positive parenting" ideas I had been bombarded with at the school.

What's wrong with "hey, Mister, you need to do more around the house?"

It was a difficult time. Ward saw me as a nag, and I completely understood why. He wasn't putting things back where they belonged—that's right, things belong in specific places. Ward's response to my criticism of his cavalier ways was often "*Who Moved My Cheese*, Kari?" In his mind, he was scolding me for being too petty. I knew he'd never read the book; he was just quoting me the title. One day hearing that comeback, I lost it.

"Ward, I spent twenty minutes this morning trying to find the vacuum attachment for furniture! Do you want to know where I found it?"

"Not really."

"In your bathrobe! Which was in a ball on top of the refrigerator!"

"What's your point?"

"I don't have twenty minutes! And that book doesn't have anything to do with nagging wives! That would be some jerky husband to write a book making fun of his wife searching frantically for stuff . . ." And then of course I started sobbing uncontrollably, just like Mary Tyler Moore in *The Dick Van Dyke Show*. "Oh, Rob!"

Ward put his arm around my shoulders, "We have to figure this out, Kid."

That's exactly what Rob Petrie would have done on *The Dick Van Dyke Show*.

We did figure it out a little bit at a time. We had also forgotten about a strategy we had come up with years before. It was a simple phrase that helped us out of some horrible arguments. When the disagreement became unproductive and opportunities for hurting each other, one of us would try to remember to shout out, "UF not FU!" (United Front not Fuck You!) It was a reminder we were on the same side and we needed to rely on each other's strengths, not our weaknesses. It was a rallying call to our better selves. We hashed out how to get back to being on the same side when we had created a wedge made of "if only" and "you always."

Ward then asked a very practical question. "I don't know what I do to bother you until it's too late, and you're mad."

Isn't that the truth? That's a whole book on the dynamics of females and males; *Uh, What Did I Do This Time?* could be the title.

"Excellent point! Act like a guy who wants to get laid. That should keep you on your best behavior!" I offered enthusiastically.

"Alright, I can try that. What are you going to do?" he countered.

"I am going to act like it's important to me that you not think I'm a bitch."

"Sounds good," he answered laughing.

Soon after, a challenge came our way we were united on. We needed to move from our triplex. Our neighborhood was changing. We had known there was likely illegal activity going on in the house across the street and ignored it until the night I walked into the living room to find Thorin standing on the couch with the shade pulled up. Outside stood an ambulance, a fire truck, a crime scene investigation unit, and three police cars. Ward talked to one of the officers. There had been a stabbing, and the victim claimed he had fallen on his knife. Somehow that didn't seem plausible to us having watched all five seasons of *The Wire*.

Thorin, Coco, and Walt hated the move so much they all tried to escape. One afternoon, I was working at the dining room table in our new apartment when I looked up from the computer and saw a woman in cut-off shorts, a halter top, and high-heeled sandals walking down the middle of street with Coco in her arms while a man with an impressive pompadour drove a Thunderbird convertible slowly behind her. I felt like I was watching a scene from a John Waters movie. I tore outside.

"Oh! Our Coco!" I yelled from our porch.

"Listen, Hon, your Coco almost got smashed by us!"

"Oh, how terrible! Thank you for getting her home!"

A week later, I was working at the computer again and looked up and out the window to see a little boy with a cowboy hat standing next to a German shepherd. I screamed, and instead of running out the front door, putting me about ten feet from where I saw them, I went to the den to check to make sure it wasn't their doppelgangers outside. I flew out the backdoor and ran to the front and around the corner where I saw them ambling side-by-side down the sidewalk.

I caught up to them quickly. I grabbed them both toward me. Thorin tried wrestling away to continue their walk. Walt looked at me as if he were saying, "Hey, where were you?"

"You're too young to leave the house alone," I explained to Thorin.

"Not lone," he smiled, pointing to Walt.

"You have to have a human with you."

Later, after deconstructing the situation with Ward, we discovered he'd left the backdoor unlocked when he left for the store, and unbeknownst to us, Thorin's physical strength was such that he now could open the door. We also realized he must have let Coco out the previous week. In addition, I had been engrossed in my work. Although Thorin was in the next room, he was unsupervised for several minutes, which immediately made me realize how children fall down wells. I was beside myself thinking about what could have happened. Getting hit by a car was at the top of the list.

"Thorin is getting stronger, that's a good thing. And, Walt is a good dog," Ward pointed out.

I wrote about that incident on the blog as well. Ward heard from another party, "Kari needs to be more careful! That was dangerous." Everybody likes to give me parenting advice.

Aside from Thorin developing muscle tone and strength, he was promoted at school from the Caterpillar Room to the Rainbow Room. I thought it was my duty to prepare him for the transition to the new classroom, which was right next door to his old classroom—not in another school or on Mars.

"There's no reason to be nervous about the Rainbow Room or the new teachers," I said to Thorin as I set down his juice. *Oh, boy! I was the nervous one!*

Thorin looked at me wide-eyed, then he covered his ears.

"No, no, no, no . . ."

Ward overheard us from the bathroom then leaned out.

"Stop talking! You're freaking him out!" he whispered.

"Who wants ice cream for breakfast?" I offered.

The distraction was enough to get Thorin back on track. Ward entered stage right, and before sitting down, he gave me the raised eyebrow look. After our ice cream breakfast, I was able to hold it together until we arrived at school.

As I walked with Thorin to the new classroom, I told him, "Oh, my, you're going to have fun today!" But I couldn't just say it once; I repeated it down the hallway. By the time we got to the doorway, he clung to me refusing to go into the classroom. I looked to the new teacher.

"What do you suggest?"

"Leave quickly," she said in a very deadpan voice, her eyes hooded.

I didn't understand why I had behaved like that until I talked to Patty at work.

"What are you really afraid of?" she asked me.

"I don't know."

"I do. The Caterpillars were divided up. Some went to the Butterfly Room, and the others went to the Rainbow Room. You asked what the difference was and you didn't feel like you got a straight answer, right?"

"Right," I replied tightly.

"What do you think the difference is?" she asked sympathetically.

Sighing I said, "I think the Rainbow Room is not as challenging. I think they're holding Thorin back."

Patty shook her head. "He doesn't get to become a butterfly."

I bit my lip. "Right."

———

I think some staff members thought we pushed Thorin, and Ward and I thought some of them had low expectations for him. Other staff never interfered at all. Several months earlier, Thorin was at a standstill with talking, and he was ignoring many instructions. The speech therapist saw it as part of his speech deficiencies and distractibility issues. I talked to Dr. Peggy, his pediatrician, and she sent us to an ear, nose, and throat doctor. Thorin needed tubes in his ear, and after a hearing test, the doctor determined Thorin was likely having difficulty hearing clearly from even a few feet away. It was also discovered Thorin had permanent, mild, bilateral hearing loss. The doctor confirmed that Thorin's poor hearing could stall his speech development and account for not following directions. The speech therapist was appropriately embarrassed and apologetic, and she referred all the children on her caseload for hearing tests.

Once his tubes were in, his speech gains were apparent to us but not as readily to the speech therapist. At home, I was secretly— unbeknownst to Thorin—writing down what he was saying. The school agreed to do the same, but the notebook was often blank. At home, he used a combination of signing and talking. He was saying things, such as "I want more, please"; "I don't want to"; "Don't want it"; "Go outside now"; "Mommy help me"; "Taking dogs out"; and "More waffles, please."

A few times, he would make observations that felt thrilling. Pointing to the stars on his pillowcase, he said the word "stars" then pointed to the ceiling and said the phrase "stars in the sky." And, during a walk, Thorin heard a bird tweeting above us in a tree. He pointed up and said, "Birdy! Birdy in tree. Hi! Birdy!"

When I told the speech therapist, she was not as impressed.

"Imagine all the thoughts he must have he can't express," I said.

No response. She just looked at me quizzically.

She then informed me Thorin couldn't follow one- and two-step tasks. I knew that wasn't true. I had no problem with him following through on three-step directions, like "Thorin, get your shoes and sweater and meet me at the door." I asked her for an example.

"I asked him to get my pencil from the shelf, and he couldn't do it."

"Shelf? Where's the shelf in this room?"

She pointed to the play kitchen.

"Why would your pencil be on that?"

"What do you mean?"

"It's an odd place. I'm guessing Thorin knew you were testing him. He doesn't like that. Maybe give him a two-step request of something you actually want. I would make it real. Also "shelf" is a funny word."

"What's so funny about it?"

"Well, I don't know if Thorin has ever heard that word."

She crossed her arms tight over her chest. I could see the conversation was frustrating for her, but I found her assessments stagey.

The disagreements with the staff didn't stop with the speech therapist. During an IEP meeting, a recommendation was made that

"Thorin will reduce the number of antagonizing behaviors to no more than once per day with no more than one teacher prompt for five days in a row." I was surprised.

"Antagonizing? What behaviors are those?"

"Well, he taps kids on the shoulder over and over again and also nudges them in the ribs with his elbow," the teacher said.

Without thinking, I said, "Oh, I know where he learned that!"

"Where?"

I knew my answer wasn't going to go over well.

"From me. He and I do that to each other to be funny."

Ward audibly groaned, garnering laughs from the group.

"The other kids don't think it's funny."

"No, of course not. I'll just tell him to stop. I'll explain it."

"There are other things, too."

"Like what?" The frustration in my voice was clear.

"It might change from day to day."

Against our better judgment, we allowed the goal to be added. An IEP meeting can elicit all kinds of emotions and confusion. Sitting with nine professionals, who are recommending what is best for Thorin, becomes exhausting, and confusion over what is fact and what is opinion becomes blurred. It wasn't until later I realized the goal— to reduce antagonizing behaviors—seemed contradictory to their positive philosophy. Wouldn't the goal have been to maximize positive interactions?

The most dramatic difference in perspective came from Thorin. At dinner one night, Thorin's eyes welled up, then tears fell down his face.

"Hey, what happened?" Ward asked, concerned.

"No," as he continued silently crying.

"Are you sick?" I reached out toward him.

"No!"

Ward went to put his arms around Thorin.

"Hey, come here," he said gently.

Thorin pulled away.

"No! Top!"

I slowly leaned in and asked, "Okay, okay, Sweetheart, did something happen?"

Thorin signed the words "scared baby."

In a soft voice Ward asked, "Who's the scared baby, Thorin?"

"Me."

I shook my head. "Thorin, you aren't a baby."

"Yes, am!"

"Thorin, what do you mean?" asked Ward.

"Kool."

"At school?"

Thorin nodded his head.

"Did someone make you scared?" Ward asked.

"No! Me!"

"You're a scared baby at school?" I asked.

He nodded yes.

"Oh, that's not good," I said.

"Done now."

"Okay, we'll talk more later," Ward offered.

"No more."

"Alright. Thanks for telling us," he told him.

"Yes. Good. Top."

Thorin got up and left the room.

After he went to bed, Ward and I marveled at what Thorin was able to tell us. We agreed we should meet with the school staff together. I talked to Louise the next day about setting up a meeting. The meeting would take place before school the following day.

I was the first to speak at the meeting.

"A couple nights ago, Thorin told us he feels like a scared baby at school. No one here did anything he just feels . . ." My voice trailed off; this was harder than I thought it would be.

I turned to Ward, and he jumped in.

"We don't think he feels like that all the time."

Why were Ward and I being so protective of their feelings instead of just describing what transpired with Thorin? Maybe they did contribute to him feeling like a scared baby.

Louise spoke up, "Thorin is always so happy! He struts around with confidence."

Yeah he's always so happy unless he is doing something antagonizing, I thought.

Ms. Deadpan, the teacher from Thorin's new classroom, said very deliberately, "How exactly how did he tell you that?"

I sensed a direct challenge, but was she questioning our credibility or Thorin's ability to communicate? I wished I had asked her that, but instead I said, "He started crying at dinner so we tried teasing out what happened. . . ."

Ward interjected, "He signed 'scared baby.' I asked him to explain and he said 'kool.'"

"That's it?" Ms. Deadpan responded.

"Well," I said, "I asked if he felt like a scared baby at school. He said yes."

"It sounds like you fed him that idea," she countered.

Ward and I looked at each other. The discussion became about the validity of our story. In their defensiveness, they were forgetting the quarterly report we had received from them the week before, stating "His peers struggle to understand Thorin and have difficulty understanding and interpreting the additional modes of communication that Thorin utilizes. Also children in play tend to move from one thing to the next rather quickly and have often moved on to the next topic while Thorin is commenting." The report also noted Thorin played alone 50 percent of the time.

Thorin feeling like a scared baby didn't seemed far-fetched to us. Under those circumstances who wouldn't feel like a scared baby? We started to wonder when did those "antagonizing behaviors" occur? Was it when the others moved on from him as he was trying to communicate? Was it being alone more often than not? Could the IEP goals have been for the staff to intervene and allow Thorin to finish his thought? So many wonderful things had happened for Thorin at the school, but the concerning things were tipping the balance. It was discouraging.

Thorin would start kindergarten in less than a year. Ward and I were concerned he would not be prepared for public school. I shared our concerns privately with Louise.

"You've got nothing to worry about. Thorin will be eligible for a self-contained classroom," Louise commented.

In essence, the self-contained classroom would be like the Rainbow Room without a cutesy name.

"Louise, we want Thorin to be in an inclusive classroom, not self-contained."

She looked surprised, "We wouldn't recommend that."

"Research shows that kids in inclusive settings do better academically and socially."

"You can actually wait on kindergarten. You can delay another year. Keep him here."

Thorin would be six, almost seven years old when he started, though. As it was, he would be almost six years old when he started kindergarten in the fall. What would lead us to believe they would start raising the bar? We were fundamentally in opposition regarding Thorin. I told Ward we needed less of them and more of something else. He agreed wholeheartedly. With only nine months before the first day of kindergarten, I started looking for a miracle school.

Within a week, I found a school. After speaking with the school director, she recommended I talk to another mother whose daughter attended the school and had Down syndrome. On the school tour, we ran into Amy and her daughter, Maggie. Ward and I stopped to chat with her, and Thorin and Maggie set off to play in the stairway.

Amy asked, "How old is he, again?

"Five."

"She's five, too. When is his birthday?"

I told Amy the date.

"That's her birthday," she replied.

Ward and I said, at the same time, "Wow!"

Amy pushed ahead rapidly asking more questions. What State was he born in? Same. City? Same. Hospital? Same.

I got goose bumps. She explained that a few hours before her daughter was born, a boy who had Down syndrome was also born at the hospital. The boy's mother was in a room three doors down from Amy. The hospital staff thought it was a great opportunity for the two moms to meet, given their mutual bond. The boy's mother said yes to the meeting and then changed her mind. Ward and I stood there with our mouths open, shaking our heads.

Amy was crushed when the mother changed her mind. "I was sure it meant something that these two babies were born within hours of each other."

"So you never saw him until now?" I asked.

"I did see him in the nursery. I went to be with Maggie but I saw him a couple cribs over, so I did go take a peek at him. He was beautiful."

It was bizarre to be meeting someone who had seen Thorin at birth. That's when I realized Maggie was part of Thorin's origin story—a story many adoptive parents never get to know.

"For the last five years, I looked on the local Down syndrome parents' webpage checking to see if a boy with that birthday had been entered. At events, I would ask people if they knew the boy. I was afraid maybe he had died."

"You had a look on your face when you started asking."

"I just had this feeling!" she said. "This sounds so strange, but when I saw him just now I did wonder. They both have blond hair, blue eyes, and they're the same size. They could be . . ."

"Twins," we all said in unison.

We scheduled the first of many play dates over the years with Maggie and her family, including birthday parties, of course.

———

We ended up not transferring Thorin to the new school, realizing it would be too disruptive for Thorin. I sat down with Louise, and we were able to move toward a common goal named Thorin. The staff would lift the bar on his developmental delays. I would restart our relationship there by being more honest. I would, however, never cotton to Ms. Deadpan. She made it clear she thought she knew what was best for Thorin. I made it clear I thought she was an annoying gnat.

———

I realized that I was asking for the bar to be raised for Thorin at school, but at home we were using covered cups because he was still throwing whatever he drank. I feared he would be in high school, drinking out of a sippy cup. It was time for tactics.

One morning at breakfast, I got up my nerve and put his juice in a child-sized coffee cup with a Santa face on the side of it; I had to steady my hand.

"Hey, here's our favorite guy, Santa!" I said as a distraction from the fact it wasn't a covered cup.

"Oh, yeah!" said Thorin.

For the next several minutes, I smugly observed Thorin drinking his juice. This was a snap! I wished I'd done it ages ago.

Ward walked into the room. "Alright! A big boy cup!"

I tried to telepathically send him a pleading message: *Ward, what are you fucking thinking? Why call attention to the cup?*

Thorin looked at us, smiled, and dropped the cup and its contents on the floor.

Thorin had been with us 1,068 days. Figuring three meals a day—omitting snack time—that represented 3,204 meals. Given those parameters, I calculated he had thrown his juice and milk, around 6,500 times. I knew it meant something. I was convinced his pools had meaning in the way Nabokov in *Bend Sinister* used puddles, ink stains, and spilled milk to reflect upon tenderness and beauty. I knew Thorin's puddles had depth but I didn't know what they reflected.

A few months later, Ward and I attended a conference for parents of children with Down syndrome. We were particularly interested because the keynote speaker was from Boston's Children's Hospital. The title of his speech was simply "Behavior." His first question to the audience was "Does your child throw things?" Ward and I leaned forward in our seats.

Next, he told the audience that behavior is communication. We learned children with delayed speech and language get upset by not being able to take part in the world of talkers, which goes something like this:

- No one realizes the sounds you are making are you talking—throw something!
- Everyone is talking to each other but not you—throw something!
- You don't know yet how to get Kyle to play with you— throw his truck!

I was right! Thorin had been telling us something! His pools had depth! Score one for Mommy! The speaker then went on to explain how to deal with the behavior in a non-judgmental way. However, my long-awaited triumph in understanding Thorin as a real mother does was short lived.

After the speaker's presentation there was a Q & A period. I had a question I was dying to ask. What seemed to me to be Thorin's ability to read my mind was still happening three years later. Keys in the toilet had just been the beginning. It was such a common occurrence I censored my thoughts, concerned he would know what I was thinking and do that thing. I would be thinking of suggesting an ice cream stop while driving in the car when Thorin would pipe up from the back to say, "Yes, want ice cream!" On more than one occasion he yelled, "Bess ou!" from the other room before I sneezed. A few weeks earlier I silently read the printing on the pajamas he was wearing. The design was series of police cars intertwined with caution tape. The text I squinted to read was: Do Not Cross Police Line. Thorin looked up at me. He then traced the line on the cloth with his finger and said very clearly: "Do not cross police line." He smiled at me as he walked away. I smiled back in a way that would not suggest I was freaked out once again.

Unbeknownst to me, Ward for the last three years had also experienced Thorin's uncanny ability to anticipate his thoughts and he, too, censored his inner voice. Perhaps equally as bafflingly as Thorin's ability, we had never talked to each other about it until a week before the conference. That day we shared numerous stories about what had transpired for the past three years. We could not identify exactly why we had never spoken of it before. We guessed maybe it was the oddity of it. But, finding ourselves listening to this behaviorist, I thought it's serendipitous. I'm supposed to ask him about IT! As he fielded questions from other parents, I figured out how to phrase my question.

I turned to Ward whispering, "I'm going to ask him about you-know-what."

He immediately knew I meant what we referred to as Thorin's ESP.

"Please don't. Don't. Don't."

"It will be okay," I reassured him. "I was right about throwing things."

"This is different. Just wait," he said as he put his hand gently on my arm.

"I have to."

"Oh, God, you don't."

My hand shot up, and the speaker pointed to me. Ward slunk low in his seat with his head down. I stood up.

"I am a little nervous here. My husband and I said we wouldn't talk to other people about this, but have you ever heard about children with Down syndrome having . . . for a lack of a better word . . . ESP? You know the ability to know things . . ."

He made a face of distaste and shook his head slowly, "No, I haven't ever heard of that."

Ward was right; it was a bad move on my part. I sat back down, painfully aware all eyes were on me in the auditorium.

Later, I was philosophical about it; I had applied special attributes to Thorin because of his Down syndrome. In the same way certain strangers suggested Thorin was an angel from God, I had mistaken Thorin's psychic abilities as a Down syndrome gift. It made me more sympathetic to people who were likewise ignorant. It was also a painful reminder I needed to be watchful of my beliefs about Down syndrome. It appeared Thorin's freaky ability was just about Thorin being Thorin, and I could count us lucky he was not like the kid in *The Shining*.

First day of Kindergarten

CHAPTER FIVE

I Hear You Knocking, but You Can't Come In

In preparation of Thorin starting kindergarten, Ward and I were notified there would be a transition meeting. Aside from us, there would be five people from Thorin's preschool; a representative from the school district's special services; a representative from Child Developmental Services; the principal of the elementary school; an occupational therapist; a physical therapist; a speech therapist; a special education teacher; and a kindergarten teacher.

We notified the elementary school that we wanted Thorin in a regular classroom. We knew from Thorin's preschool and child services that the request was going to be challenged by the school, but we tried to keep a positive vibe. The preschool staff still did not believe he should be in a regular classroom, but they agreed not to share that information at the meeting. It helped that I had a romanticized vision of the school building, which reminded me of a mini-version of the fictitious Walt Whitman High School from the 1970s TV show *Room 222*. Freaking Walt Whitman!

"Maybe this is a good omen! Walt Whitman High was a very groovy, progressive school," I told Ward.

"I hope you're right," he offered not exactly with enthusiasm.

The meeting took place in one of the classrooms. We sat at tables arranged in a square, making it feel like a collaborative space. After introductions were made—which took a while given the number of participants—the kindergarten teacher said in a dismissive, hostile voice, "He shouldn't be in my classroom."

WTF! She had never met Thorin!

I looked at Ward; his mouth was open.

"Hey, can you say that?" I asked her. I looked around for clarification from the room. I didn't think she could say that legally based on federal law and the least restrictive environment clause, not to mention common decency. Most of the people in the room had their head down. Thorin's physical therapist from the preschool— bless her heart—shook her head no. Ward and I turned toward the principal, who was looking at her phone.

The kindergarten teacher ignored my question and continued. "Kindergarten has changed quite a bit in the last forty years. It's more cognitively challenging. I don't see him keeping up."

Her statement seemed implausible as well as a not so veiled dig at my age. Were they splitting the atom in kindergarten now?

"Are any students with disabilities in regular classrooms?" I asked.

The teacher was seething. "Not with his profile, no."

The blessed physical therapist spoke. "When I started decades ago, I had students in regular classrooms. It wasn't a big deal. It was done. And, school hasn't changed that much."

"Thank you!" I said, beaming, while Ward nodded to her and made the thumbs-up sign.

The special services person from the district ignored her comment, instead asking the kindergarten teacher, "What are you recommending?"

"We see him in the developmental classroom," she said, gesturing toward the special education teacher.

As if on well-rehearsed cue, the special education teacher joined the conversation.

"My students have their own classroom. They do come up for the specials—art and music. At those times, they're with the regular students."

"Come up from where?" Ward asked.

"Their classroom is in the basement," she replied.

At the word *basement*, I felt like I had entered a time warp. I saw Monty—the young man from my youth who was in the church basement—hidden away. Then, I saw Thorin who would never make it to the Walt Whitman High fantasy of *Room 222*. I shook inside.

Ward and I were adamant: this was unacceptable. The meeting became a stalemate, and the woman from the district suggested we end the meeting and scheduled a continuation for the following month. When Ward and I got home, we were equally furious.

"Why was that kindergarten teacher so angry?" Ward practically yelled.

"I don't know! Why was she allowed to say those things? It's so blatant."

"Because it's business as usual. A lot of parents probably say, 'Thank you for telling me where so-and-so should be.'"

We decided not to make the same mistake of waiting too long to say what needed to be said. We agreed I would speak to the principal. Unfortunately, she didn't return my phone calls. The next time I called, I asked the receptionist what time the principal was scheduled to arrive the following day. At the appointed time, Thorin and I roamed the staff parking lot, waiting for her. She was quite surprised to see us, but, to her credit, she pretended to be happy about it. I think it helped she had her son with her, who was a student at the same school. She suggested we walk to the playground. Once there, Thorin took off to explore, and her son found his friends. I started our conversation.

"I love your school. I could picture Thorin here—but in a regular classroom."

"We'd love to have him." As she said that, we both noticed—at the same moment—her son asking Thorin if he needed help climbing the stairs. Thorin shyly nodded yes, and the boy gently supported his back as he took each step.

"Your son is thoughtful."

"Thank you," she smiled.

"Okay, about the transition meeting for Thorin. I don't understand why the kindergarten teacher was allowed to say he shouldn't be in her classroom?"

"Oh, I wished I'd been at that meeting!"

"What? You were at the meeting."

"I was?"

"Yes. Yes, you were. You recognized me just now in the parking lot because I met you at the meeting." I felt like I had been dropped into a Joseph Heller novel.

"When was the meeting?"

"Last week."

"So, she said that?"

"Yes."

"Why don't I remember that?"

I sensed I was seconds away from chocolate-covered cotton balls.

She wasn't going to fess up to it so I said, "I don't know, but can we talk about a regular classroom right now?"

"I don't think that's a good idea. That's the kind of thing I like to leave up to my staff."

When I called Ward, he yelled, "She lied! This is a conspiracy!"

If Ward's passionate outcry had been made by a character in a John Grisham novel, I would have agreed and said, "Yes! Let's take her down!" But, there was no documentation that the teacher had made the statement "he shouldn't be in my classroom." We didn't tape the meeting, and if the principal was saying she didn't hear it, how many others would follow suit? In my mind, Grisham had an easier time constructing complicated plot lines than we did living them.

"Let's figure out Plan B," I suggested to Ward.

——

A family from Thorin's preschool had a son, David, who also had Down syndrome. He had been attending another elementary school an equal distance from our house and was in a regular classroom. I talked to his mom about the school; she was enthusiastic and positive. She gave me a great deal of information about the school, including the fact the classrooms were wired with state-of-the-art amplification.

We would have to make the case for an out-of-neighborhood school transfer for Thorin. We knew we couldn't make it based on the other child with Down syndrome. But, we could make a case that Thorin would be better served in a state-of-the-art acoustic facility with his mild hearing loss.

First, I found out the name of the system they used at the school. I spoke with a technology person from the company, and he was beyond excited to have a real-live person talk to him about the wonders of his product. I probably could have gotten off the phone fifteen minutes earlier than necessary, but he was just so thrilled. He directed me to several research articles based on product data and those written by independent evaluators. What he had shared was confirmed by all the data I found: the system benefited students with distractibility issues and mild hearing loss—evidence of both had been well documented by Thorin's teachers and specialists.

Then I sent the information to Thorin's ear, nose, and throat doctor who, after reviewing the research, agreed to write a letter of support for Thorin to attend the out-of-neighborhood school. Days later, as I compiled my last pack of documentation for each meeting attendee, Ward suggested we all go out to dinner to celebrate my braininess. I felt, in a little way, like Julia Roberts in *The Pelican Brief*.

At the transition meeting, part two, we completely sidestepped the request for a regular classroom and asked for an out-of-neighborhood placement. I presented my data and referred the attendees to various texts that I had thoughtfully highlighted for them.

Check-fucking-mate!

Grumbling and futile attempts were made to rebut the request. The kindergarten teacher glared at me during most of the meeting. I wrote a note on my paper—covering it so only Ward could see it— which read "She's such an asshat," and I added an arrow so Ward would know which person I was talking about.

He scribbled over my note and wrote above it: "Stick to the script!"

When the meeting adjourned, it looked as if we won the battle.

Summer started two weeks after our request for the out-of-neighborhood school transfer. During those summer months, two major developments occurred: potty training and moving my mom to Maine.

First, I tackled potty training head-on. Thorin was still having accidents, so he wore pull-ups. I had friends whose children with Down syndrome were potty trained at age two, others at seven, and some in between. Thorin was five years old and wasn't potty trained mostly because of me.

When I found out from the preschool teacher I should have Thorin wear underwear and expect accidents, I was horrified. I wanted to wrap everything in plastic, especially me. Just let him pee on the furniture? That was Coco's job. I couldn't have two beings urinating all over the house at once. Thorin was pooping in the toilet, but I was convinced it was because it was a better venue to showcase his productions than a pull-up. I was floored the first time he called me into the bathroom to view his poop. He gestured with his hands much like a game show assistant revealing a prize and then said, "Ta-da!"

I had heard about a clinic called Potty University. Like any sought-after educational institution, it was extremely hard to get into it. I knew our child services caseworker had a few slots for clients, so I called her and explained the situation. She was terrific.

"Yes, you can have one of the slots for Thorin! Anything for my little surfer dude!" At the time, Thorin's hair was down to his shoulders.

First, I met with Courtney, the social worker at Potty University while the receptionists fell over themselves entertaining Thorin. I described the situation briefly without going into my shortcomings or my suspicions about him. I also didn't mention that the day before he had stripped everything off our bed and pissed all over it after I had, moments earlier, told him about Potty University.

"What do you think is the major issue?" she asked.

"I think it's me."

"Good, that will makes this much easier. Do you think Thorin is in a power struggle with you?"

"Yes, I think it could be something like that." I didn't think it was much of a struggle, though, considering he was winning.

Next, Courtney went over the Potty University protocol. Then, she brought Thorin into the office with us. She read a book to him about using the potty that included a section on sneaky poops, which are the ones that happen when you don't listen to your body. Thorin solemnly nodded at the description. I could see he was taking this seriously. Then Courtney brought out a stuffed animal turtle named Thomas. Thomas pooped out some turds into a small plastic toilet. She had Thorin push the tiny handle so it would flush.

"Should I buy that book and get a Thomas turtle?" I asked her.

"No, I already read it to him, and he just saw Thomas poop," which sounded more like "I'll tell you when I want you to do something."

Later when I told Ward about Thomas, I failed to mention he was a toy. Ward was amazed and asked how she taught a turtle to poop on command.

Courtney gave us forms to record Thorin's progress and had him pick out stickers to track his successes. If he earned enough stickers by the end of the week, he could pick a special prize.

"Get your mom to take you shopping for underpants," she told Thorin.

"So soon?" I asked.

"Keeping him in pull-ups tells him you don't think he can do this. He can do it. He will do it."

When I saw Thorin nodding his head in agreement like a dutiful cult member, I knew Courtney must be The Pee Whisperer.

Within a couple weeks, there were no more accidents. Thorin received a diploma from Potty University, which he and I were very proud of. First mission of the summer accomplished. Thorin would start kindergarten potty trained!

Next Betty and I had finally convinced our eighty-year-old mom to move from her hometown in Wisconsin to Maine. Her decision was based on two key factors. One reason was regrettable; her health was failing, and she knew she would need more help. The second reason was joyous; she wanted to spend the time she had left with Thorin, who had become her best friend.

In the three years since we had Thorin, we made many trips to Wisconsin. My mom had also started coming to our house for a couple months at a time. A friend of hers told me, "Your mom all but rolled her eyes when any of us talked about our grandkids. Then Thorin came on the scene, and he was the only thing she talked about."

My mom shared with me that being Thorin's Bubba was the role of a lifetime. I think in Wisconsin she had great friends, many for over sixty years and a few longer than that, but she didn't have a meaning for her life. Thorin was her meaning. A few weeks before Thorin started school, she moved into her own apartment at a senior complex, ten minutes away from us.

After my mom settled in, she wanted to take Thorin shopping for school clothes. When the three of us went anywhere in the car, my mom and Thorin sat in the backseat and didn't hear anything I said. My mom would share things with him, such as "When your mom was a little girl playing a game, she would cry like a baby if she didn't win" or "She ran around the neighborhood naked once." *What the hell?* No one was talking about losing or being naked. Thorin would laugh and offer a sympathetic sigh at her challenges with me. On those occasions, I wished my car had the dark-tinted glass partition afforded a chauffeur.

Picking the proper school attire required a discussion for every selection. Each of us was equally invested, and the two of them were a voting block. While at Old Navy, I pulled out a child size Hawaiian wedding shirt in espresso with white embroidery.

"I love this!" I exclaimed and showed them the shirt.

"Okay. Where would he go in that?" my mom asked skeptically.

"Where?" echoed Thorin, making a frowny face.

"School," I said, trying to sound confident.

"He's getting his haircut before school, right?"

Thorin looked up at her while petting her hand. "Hair, Mommy?"

"Thorin, who are you talking to?" I asked.

"To Bubba-Mommy," he replied. Then he and Bubba-Mommy hugged and kissed each other for what seemed like thirty seconds.

My mom must have felt sorry for me because she said, "Thorin, I think we should let her get the shirt for you. Would you wear it, Beautiful?"

"Yesith! Yesith! Yesith!"

⸻

The start of the school year arrived, and Ward and I took Thorin to school for his first day of kindergarten. I asked Thorin if I could help put his outfit together.

"Let see," he said.

"How about the cool brown shirt Bubba let me get with these madras shorts and your brown sandals?"

What I really wanted to do was dress him in coat of armor. I was scared about the first day of kindergarten for regular reasons and Thorin reasons. Would kids comment on how he looked? Could

I dazzle them with styling so they wouldn't judge him based on almond-shaped eyes?

"Do you like the outfit?"

Thorin smiled. "Yesith. Good, Mommy."

"How are you feeling about today?"

"No."

"No talking about it."

"No talking."

Ward pulled me aside before the three of us left the house.

"No crying until we say goodbye to him at the school and we are out of his eye sight."

"I know that; my mom already told me."

Thorin's teacher, Ms. Charles, was standing outside the door of the school waiting for her class.

"Hi Thorin! I'm so excited to see you!"

Thorin promptly ran to me, hugging me tightly as he said, "No Mommy! Tay! Tay!"

Ward shook his head no and made an exaggerated smile.

As I gently peeled Thorin off my body, I said in the sunniest voice I could muster, "No, Honey. You go with Ms. Charles! You're okay."

Ms. Charles reached out. "You can come over and hug me."

She already had three huggers grabbing her tightly when Thorin joined them. Ward led me away.

"Stop looking at him. There's no reason to look at him."

I didn't make it to the car but I was around the other side of the building when I started sobbing. Ward put his arms around me. I looked up at him, and his eyes were wet.

"You, too?"

Smiling, he said, "Hey, I'm not made of stone. And, look around here."

Ward gestured toward other parents who were sitting in their car and wiping away tears or blowing their noses. It was an emotional day for all the kindergarten parents.

At the end of the day, I met Thorin's aide, Mrs. Louise, whom Thorin had immediately starting calling Lo-Lo. She shared with me that Thorin was one of the children who volunteered for show-and-share. There was some confusion about what he was saying, but they were able to figure enough of it out. I was elated. He had never done anything like that before. It was a great start.

Our work schedules didn't align with the school hours, so I enrolled Thorin in the city's before- and after-school recreation program located at the school. We needed coverage, but it was another change added to already long list of changes. For more than two years, Thorin was in a small school with nine children in the class. In kindergarten, he was one of twenty-two students, and at the recreation program, he was one of thirty-four children. Also, Thorin was literally the smallest child in the school. Kids—always girls— would stop to say how cute he was. It was clear he wasn't cute in a dreamy way but in a tiny child way.

———

Two weeks into the school year, Thorin started having bathroom accidents. I called The Pee Whisperer, who was her ever-efficient self.

"Have them use the protocol I gave you. It's a normal response to stress. He's facing a lot of changes. Tell them not to make a big deal of it."

A week later, Thorin became known as "The Hitter" in his class as well as "The Scratcher" and "The Screamer," but thankfully the last two were constrained to the recreation program. In both areas, he received time-outs, which made things more frustrating for

Thorin. When I probed about the hitting in the classroom, I was told it was more like poking and pushing.

"Okay, still not okay, but let's not refer to it as 'hitting' anymore. Has Thorin hurt anyone?"

The person laughed and said, "No."

"What's going on when it happens?"

"He's trying to get someone's attention."

That sounded annoying but not aggressive to me.

Later, I asked a staff person with the recreation program about the situation there.

"When is the scratching and screaming happening? What happens before it?"

"Someone else is scratching or screaming."

"It's imitative?"

"Oh, maybe!"

"Let's assume it is. Has he broken skin?"

Laughing, she replied, "No."

Although he wasn't viewed as aggressive, it was clear Thorin was seen as having behavioral problems. Thorin needed support with his new challenges, and we knew he was frustrated, but it was difficult for him to articulate what he needed. I decided to call The Pee Whisperer, who referred us to her colleague, Dr. Rachel.

Dr. Rachel was a lovely woman and not at all concerned about Thorin's behavior after observing him in the classroom. She explained, "Behavior is communication. Thorin's using these tactics to get attention because he has difficulty speaking and being understood." I felt like I should have "behavior is communication" tattooed on my wrist.

She gave the school staff the following recommendations: refrain from giving Thorin consequences and help him convey his feelings and thoughts. Dr. Rachel billed the insurance by giving Thorin a diagnosis of "disruptive behavior disorder," which would later become a concern for Ward and me.

———

With all of these distractions, we missed the fact Thorin was stealing the school blind. I think it was around the second week of school when he came home with a red sweatshirt that was not his. I was so used to being judged by professionals about my parenting abilities my first thought was, *What the hell? They didn't think I dressed him in enough layers?*

I took the sweatshirt back the next morning and explained, "We do not need this. Thank you!"

On a daily basis, I was pulling clothes out of his backpack and returning them. I was feeling totally judged through the articles of clothing they were giving Thorin. I was a confused when I found a pink, frilly top in his backpack. *Why on earth do they think he needs that?*

Ward finally figured it out when he picked up Thorin from school one day and noticed he was cramming a sweater that wasn't his into his backpack. Then it clicked: All the clothing he brought home hadn't been given to him. He was taking it!

Ward asked, "Have you been taking things that aren't yours?"

"Yesith!"

"Thorin you can't do that."

"Yesith, can."

"Okay, yes you have been. But you have to stop now."

Holy crap! How could I tell "them" that "The Hitter, Scratcher, Screamer" was also "The Klepto"? The next day I explained to the staff what we thought had been going on. They found the confusion mildly amusing and shared an observation they found puzzling. Thorin always seemed to be pulling things out of the lost-and-found box in the hall, insisting they were his. I assured them we were working on it.

As his thievery came to an end, I brought suspicion on myself the following month. I had agreed to volunteer at a weekend school event to try to engage with other mothers. It wasn't like these women were The Real Housewives of Portland, Maine, exactly, but they weren't what you could call friendly. During my volunteer shift, I was supposed to greet people coming in and hand them a flyer on the day's events. Next to me were two racks filled with clothing. I assumed it was a clothing giveaway, so I started picking clothes that would fit Thorin. I had a pile going. One of the mothers came over to check in with me.

When she saw my stack of clothes, she said, "Wow! You found a lot in there."

"I hope my son likes them."

"Ah, that's lost-and-found clothing."

I started laughing nervously. "Oh, I misunderstood! I thought they were free clothes!"

She looked at me blankly.

"This must look funny—not ha-ha funny—but weird funny. I'm putting these back right now!" At that moment, I totally related to Thorin's confusion about the lost and found.

———

As the school year progressed, we were encouraged by things happening at school. One morning, in particular, I had brought Thorin to school late so I walked him to his classroom. I thought I could quickly sneak him in and dash out. We entered the classroom, as quietly as possible, but one kid turned around and yelled, "Thorin!"

Bedlam ensued. Twenty-two kindergartners rose as one and ran toward us. I instinctively grabbed Thorin and backed up closer to the door. Screaming his name, they descended upon him. Ms. Charles and Lo-Lo flew into action—each calling out things, such as "Stop! Back to your seats!"

But, the kindergartners didn't stop. He soon became lost in a huddle of five- and six-year-olds. I couldn't see his face at one point and joined the other two adults in pulling the kids off him. Everyone settled back down after much direction by Ms. Charles: "No more! Let him sit down. Stop touching him. We're going to get going again." Thorin made his way to his desk and sat down. I never left my spot by the door.

Lo-Lo walked back to me. Smiling she said, "Overwhelming isn't it?"

I nodded. "I guess any change really throws kids, huh?"

"Not changes, Thorin. That happens all the time."

Without thinking I blurted, "Holy crap! He's like Elvis!"

This made Ward and me feel relieved. We had worried about bullying, but instead Thorin was treated like a rock star. We assumed Thorin felt the same way about it.

———

I left the executive-director position at the film festival. I needed a job that was less demanding so I could focus more time on Thorin. I became a parent coach for a company that had previously sold a penile enhancement product. Yes, gross. On the face of, it seemed like a bad idea, but I did agree with the tenants of the parenting program they were now hawking. I was good at my job, and it was nice being a cog in a wheel rather than the wheel. My supervisor was in her thirties and said things such as, "Let's co-create that idea."

In an attempt to engage at the school, I volunteered to head up a parents' advisory committee that was in need of a chair. The principal thanked me profusely. I was making a positive impression!

At our first meeting, we discussed areas we could develop for more support. I had an immediate thought that could help build inroads for Thorin and other children with disabilities at the school.

"I have an idea! What if we had a disability committee that did outreach and events just like the diversity committee does?"

It was as if I asked if anyone wanted to drop acid. No one responded. I was shocked.

"Um, no one thinks that's a good idea?" I continued.

Finally, the principal said, "We don't need that. We're doing fine."

A parent I had earlier pegged as a brownnoser chimed in, "I think we do a great job!"

I felt alone and could only imagine how Thorin felt at school. These same parents who were so careful in their approach to race and multiculturalism had unilaterally decided they were doing just fine with disabilities.

A few weeks later, Ms. Brownnoser and I pulled up to school at the same time. While we waited for our kids to get out, she leaned her head in our car. In a loud voice usually reserved for hard of hearing kittens, she said, "Hi Thorin! Are you unbuckling yourself? Can you unbuckle your seat belt?" Then she clapped her hands together enthusiastically—twice. I wanted to key her car or put sugar in her gas tank. She couldn't hear how demeaning she sounded and, in fact, thought she was being nice to a "Down syndrome boy."

There was another mother whose daughter was in Thorin's class. She constantly talked about how much her daughter liked Thorin.

I wondered if she really wanted me to thank her for raising such an open-minded daughter, or maybe she was angling for a college reference down the road.

One afternoon, I was waiting for Thorin after school. She came over to me.

"Last night Jordan told us again how much she likes Thorin."

"Wow. Maybe they'll get married," I said.

"What? Oh, you're funny!"

"I am funny."

I stayed silent after that. I honestly couldn't think of anything to say to her, but she did.

"I understand why Thorin pushes other kids; it's because of his communication issues."

I felt tears sting my eyes. I nodded my head and continued looking forward. She finally walked away. She must have also known he loved the Avengers. Almost everything he wore was Avenger branded, but she didn't ever say anything, such as "I guess Thorin is a real fan of the Hulk."

I knew nothing about this woman's life that might come under the heading of personal information. Had I, I certainly wouldn't have mentioned it.

⁂

A few days later, Ward was watching the news.

"Hey get out here and see this! They keep repeating it."

We stood side-by-side in the den, watching what was being touted as an inspirational story. A teenager with Down syndrome, who was the ball boy for his school's basketball team, was allowed to play as the game was winding down. A member from the opposing team threw him the ball during the game. That was the whole story.

"What do you think?" Ward asked.

"Well, he knows the kid shouldn't have thrown the ball to him."

"Yes! And what's up with letting him play? Like they did him a favor."

"They feel sorry for him. Why's that news?"

"Pity is trending today, I guess."

We both noticed a couple Facebook friends of ours had posted the story on their newsfeed. I wondered if pity would be good enough for their children rather than the genuine experience of being included as an equal. I reached out to those friends on Facebook, explaining how Ward and I saw the story. Both exchanges were terrific—they understood what our concerns were for Thorin and deleted the post. I also wondered if I would have found the story inspirational if Thorin wasn't our son.

To help process my thoughts, I wrote about it on the blog. I suggested to my readers that these types of stories seemed to suggest that when those of us without Down syndrome demonstrate some little speck of contrived humanity to people with Down syndrome, we deserve to be applauded for our efforts. I wanted so much more for Thorin. In the grand scheme of what we have to offer each other as human beings, these acts were crumbs.

Given work commitments, Ward had stopped writing on the blog in 2010 while I had continued. I still wrote storytelling posts about our family. I also wrote about my political awakening through not only Thorin's stories but also the stories of others.

One story in particular sickened me and hit hard at my greatest fears for Thorin—being victimized. On January 12, 2013, a young man named Ethan Saylor had been killed by three off-duty sheriff's deputies moonlighting as security guards at a movie theater in Maryland. Ethan had Down syndrome. He refused to leave the theater when the film he saw ended; he wanted to watch it again. The three men brought him violently to the ground, then they restrained him by his wrists and ankles with a third set of handcuffs used to connect the other sets. They laid him on his stomach, and he died of asphyxiation. The position in which he was detained was not allowed by law enforcement because of the probability of death.

My heart pounded, and I felt anxious as I hit publish on my first post about Ethan. I was Thorin's mother writing about another mother's son. In that post, I saw Ethan's death as a human rights violation. I questioned whether they would have responded likewise to someone without Down syndrome. Clearly, there had to have been an alternative to killing someone over the price of a movie ticket. The press coverage I read seemed to blame Ethan's Down syndrome for his death rather than a homicidal overreaction by the three individuals who killed him. Another author suggested that people with Down syndrome are predisposed to being stubborn. He contended Ethan might have contributed to his own death by responding in that stereotypically Down syndrome manner. I found that reasoning to be repugnant and victim blaming.

Ward and I had both heard that children with Down syndrome were stubborn. We heard that from professionals and regular folk, including parents who had children with Down syndrome. Even Lo-Lo had asked me once.

"I've been reading about Down syndrome because of Thorin. Do you think he's stubborn?"

"I think I'm stubborn."

She laughed. "I don't believe it either."

"I think Thorin processes information slower than I do, so his reaction time is slower than mine but close to the same rate as Ward. I know I look like a whirling blender to them."

All together, I wrote three posts on Ethan in March of that year. In each, I challenged the mainstream's take on his death and also the position of some of the national Down syndrome organizations. It was being written off by most as a misunderstanding with entirely too much sympathy given to the officers. At the time, I was delving into Twitter to share my posts, moving beyond my blog. A communications person from the Special Olympics contacted me to compliment me on my writing and added me to a list of disability advocates. He also shared with me it was Lawrence Downes, from the Editorial Board at the *New York Times*, who had recommended my blog to him. As I read that private message alone in our dining room, I started yelling. I had a fan who worked at the *New York Times!* I soon connected with Downes via email, and to this day, he remains a valued champion of my writing.

As fearful as I was about sticking my neck out, I knew I must be on the right track.

Ward and I had attended another conference geared for parents of children who had Down syndrome. The revelation at this one was augmentative and alternative communication (AAC) systems. We didn't know there were applications used on iPads that helped people communicate. We talked to the presenter afterward, and she recommended the Proloquo2Go application; it was easy, and children found it fun. She thought it would be a great bridge to talking in the same way signing had been. We purchased the software and an iPad, the mini version, for Thorin.

Thorin used Proloquo2Go on his iPad at home for communicating if he got stuck or if he was trying to explain how he felt. It also came in quite handy when I got a call from the school that Thorin had tried to bite a classmate. Given that he still didn't have his front teeth, the extent of the damage was a little wet mark on the girl's jeans. What the teacher told me was from the girl's point of view, but I needed to hear Thorin's side. Using the program, Thorin was able to tell me the girl was "mean," "happy," and "smiling," which made him angry enough to try to bite her. It took me a minute to realize he had described teasing.

"Thorin did she say or do anything that bothered you?"

"Yesith!"

"Can you show me what?"

"No, can't."

"Thorin I want to help. Did she say something or do something?"

"Say."

I tried moving forward, but he was stuck on how to tell me what she said. I pulled back as he got more upset. I was convinced there was a rationale for his behavior. I told him if someone bothered him, he should walk away and get help from an adult. Biting was not okay.

Ward and I realized that Thorin's classmates might not know anything about him except for his behavior and his Down syndrome. He had stopped participating in show-and-share soon after the school year started because he was frustrated with not being understood. I asked Thorin if he wanted me to go in with him to do a presentation about himself for the class using Proloquo2Go. I got an enthusiastic, "Yesith!" I made arrangements with Ms. Charles who was thrilled.

Thorin and I rehearsed our presentation in front of Ward. Thorin decided which buttons he would share—name, birthday, sister's name, dogs' names, and friends' names. He also wanted his class to know he liked flying in airplanes. After rehearsal, Ward clapped and gave Thorin feedback: "Great, Thorin! Have fun tomorrow!" As for me, he suggested Thorin and I not dress alike for the presentation.

The afternoon prior to the presentation, I had to fulfill my duties as a parent volunteer in the computer lab with Thorin's class. I found this volunteering much more rewarding than the committee. Being around twenty-one kindergartners who do not have Down syndrome made me realize something I already believed but did not always know: Thorin is not that different.

Ms. Charles gave strict instructions as she left me alone with half the class: "Everyone, only do math games on the computer." Other than a boy dressed in a sweater vest and tie, they all logged on other programs. I tried to sound cheerful and fun, "Did you hear Ms. Charles? Only math games, right?" For my efforts to stick the rules, students rolled their eyes and gave not-so-subtle side glances to each other.

One little girl asked sweetly for my help. I sat with her, feeling ever so helpful. But, I quickly realized she must have drawn the short straw to distract me while several of the others goofed off playing non-math games. I was betrayed.

I was also treated to the most unrepentant farting, ever. They were all farting with impunity. One kid's atomic fart prompted me to ask, "Say, do you think you have to go to the bathroom or something?" But what I wanted to say was "Dude! Did you just shart your pants?"

Interacting with Thorin's class also helped me figure out which girl Thorin tried to bite. In the course of ten minutes, a couple kids almost punched her, and three kids moved away from her. She absolutely did not deserve to get saliva on her pants leg, but I did want to warn her things would be much worse at the women's correctional facility later in life.

I finished my computer lab duties and headed to Thorin's classroom. As Thorin and I sat next to each other, waiting to be introduced for our presentation, I whispered in his ear.

"I'm nervous!"

"Me, too!" he whispered.

The Star of the Day, Ferrell, walked to the front of the class with us. Ferrell placed the iPad under a document camera that projected it to a screen. Thorin hit the first button. The computer-programmed boy voice said, "I use an iPad to talk." The room erupted in squeals of excitement. Thorin ran through the repertoire pretty much as rehearsed. With each button he pressed, the feedback from the kids was immediate.

"I didn't know you had a sister, Thorin!"

"What? He has a dog named Walt!"

"Your best friend's name is Ella!"

In preparing, I hadn't planned on what the reaction would be. Each piece of information delighted them. Thorin was radiant. It was—in a word—a moment. And if you do indeed see your life flash before you when you die, this will be one of my moments.

Everybody in the class wanted their picture taken and placed into the program. More squeals ensued after each corresponding name was entered and listened to. As I was packing up, Ferrell came over to me.

"So that's Thorin's iPad?"

"Yes."

"Only his, right? He uses it whenever he wants?"

"Yes."

"Do you use it?"

"No."

"I can't touch my mom's Kindle. Wow. Thorin is so lucky."

Two months later Thorin was accused of biting again. A small group of children were left alone for a couple minutes. When Ms. Charles came back, two boys said that Thorin had bitten them. She didn't give me their names but she did call their parents to let them know what happened.

"He doesn't have front teeth."

"There were no marks."

When we got home from school, I asked Thorin if we could use the iPad to talk about what happened. He said yes.

"Ms. Charles said you bit someone. Did you?"

"Yesith," he said.

I made a button in the program for Thorin that read "I bite people when I feel ___" and asked Thorin to pick an emotion to fill in the blank. He picked "afraid" and "sick."

He motioned he was hit in the face. Because the students' photos were in his program, he was able to identify who hit him: Isaiah and Christopher. He also pointed to a girl named Felicia who made a funny face at him, showing a lot of teeth. I believed him.

I emailed what I had discovered to Ms. Charles and asked if this scenario sounded plausible. She wrote back, confirming that the incident did involve those two boys and that Felicia did make funny faces.

I knew Christopher was in the recreation program with Thorin, so I started hanging around at the end of the day before I took Thorin home. A few days into my stakeout, I saw Christopher come up behind Thorin, who was standing on a platform about two feet off the ground. Had I known what he was capable of, I would have yelled to try to stop what happened next: Christopher looked around then shoved Thorin off the platform. Thorin face-planted and immediately started crying. I was shocked by Christopher's audacity and ran over to help Thorin.

I turned to Christopher and said, "I saw that!"

"It was an accident!"

"No, it was not. I want you to listen to me very carefully. Don't ever do anything like that again. Do you read me, Christopher?"

He looked like he was going to cry but held it together. It almost made me feel bad for threating a six-year-old.

I reported what happened to the staff. At first Christopher lied, then he thought better of it after he looked at me. Even at his age, he could discern the look that said, "Don't mess with me."

"I did it! I pushed him."

When I told Ward that night he said, "Kari! He's six!"

"So is Thorin. I'm a mother, Baby."

In light of my recent observations, I made more time in my schedule for shadowing Thorin before and after school. The first morning yielded tons of distressing information. Everything was fine until the morning bell rang for the kids to file into school; I witnessed nine children—in almost as many minutes—force their unsolicited help onto Thorin. He would shake his head or say no, but they didn't pay attention.

One kid scooped up Thorin's backpack and grabbed Thorin's arm to shove it in the strap. I intervened and said, "Hey, you, stop!"

The next one grabbed Thorin's hand to pull him toward the door. I took his hand off Thorin saying, "Don't touch him!"

All the way inside the building, I ran interference. A kid flew in front of me and tried to drag Thorin up the stairs, so I yelled, "Okay, I do not like that! Let go now!"

Eventually, I was able to usher Thorin to the classroom without any interruption. But once there, a boy tried to pull off Thorin's backpack, and I admonished him. "What are you doing? Move away, now!"

A girl started yelling, "He has to line up outside the door," then she pushed him in line. I got between them.

"You aren't in line, Bossy! Hey, I'm talking to you!" I said facing the girl.

Then, I turned around and found a boy holding either side of Thorin's face saying, "Do you understand?"

I peeled the boy's hands from Thorin's face.

"Don't touch him!" I said, close to tears. I felt totally discombobulated.

As quickly as it started, it was over as soon as they filed into the classroom. Thorin casually waved goodbye. Walking away, I realized I had witnessed his daily routine.

At dinner that night, Ward and I talked to Thorin about the other students.

"I saw how you're treated at school. How you feel about that?" I asked.

Thorin slammed his fork down on the table. He made jabbing and smashing gestures and said, "Mad!" He quickly amended it, "Hulk mad!"

I felt like a complete asshole for not knowing the degree to which he was managed by other children.

Ward asked, "When the kids get excited to see you, how do you feel?"

"Mad! Not baby!"

"It makes you feel like a baby, Thorin?" I asked.

"Yes! Thorin not baby!"

"That's right, Thorin. You aren't a baby," Ward replied.

"Hey, can you and I do another presentation together to tell your class how you feel?"

"Yay!"

There were only a couple weeks left of kindergarten, but we had to do something. Ward and I found it difficult to understand how this had been allowed to happen; however, it was a window into Thorin's behavior issues. He was controlling his actions much more than his peers, and I knew I didn't have the strength and restraint he demonstrated. The next day, I informed Ms. Charles we were doing another presentation. She was again enthusiastic.

In preparation, Thorin and I discussed what buttons to create in Proloquo2Go. He had several recommendations: "Wait"; "Ask me"; "Stop"; "I am mad"; and "I want to hit." Then I made recommendations, which he approved: "I don't need help" and "You do not understand me, but I understand you."

I was nervous about the presentation. What if one of them asked about Down syndrome? I didn't feel equipped to answer that line of questioning. We had not yet talked to Thorin about Down syndrome, which in retrospect seems completely ignorant on our part. If we thought it was great, why wouldn't we share that with Thorin?

When we finished our presentation, Ms. Charles asked if there were any questions. A boy's hand shot up. Thorin pointed to him saying, "Michael." In my head, I was convinced Michael was going to ask about Down syndrome. I started to panic.

Michael started to ask, "Thorin, Thorin, um, Thorin? Yeah, Thorin, I just want to know why . . . yeah . . . why . . ."

While Michael tried to find the right words, I was thinking, *Spit it out! I know you want to ask about Down syndrome.*

"Yeah . . . um . . . Thorin . . . Thorin . . . why you like Captain America so much?"

With school ending soon, I started making arrangements for Thorin to attend summer school. We knew six other classmates of his were also attending. I went to meet with the principal.

"How do we go about getting Thorin enrolled in summer school?"

"He can't go to summer school here," she replied sharply.

"Why?" I was honestly shocked.

"We don't do inclusive summer school programming here."

"Wait . . . So what happens? Where is Thorin supposed to go?"

The principal mentioned another school. "He'll be in a self-contained classroom."

I could feel myself getting upset, "But it would be better if he was with classmates . . . here. This is his school."

"No, not during the summer."

For all the little steps toward inclusion, this was a huge move backward. Thorin was clearly not like the other students, who were always included.

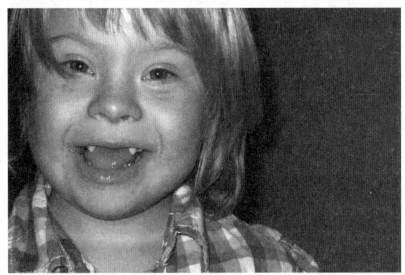

Thorin and Jade

CHAPTER SIX

We've Crossed Over to the Twilight Zone

*S*hortly after meeting with the principal, Ward and I attended an end of year IEP meeting. We learned the principal couldn't actually make the decision for Thorin's summer school placement outside of an IEP, but she still insisted he should be in a special education classroom. When the issue of Thorin's behavior came up, his physical therapist offered information she had not shared all year: "Thorin's early attempts to make physical contact with people were heavy-handed due to low tone and lack of muscle grading and perceived as hitting; then all the attention that hitting gets leads to more. So the point is Thorin needs to be taught how to touch someone gently."

"We've never heard that explanation before. Is that in your report?" I asked hoping it wasn't too late for this information to be distributed to other staff members.

"I haven't written it yet, but, yes, I will include increasing work on proprioceptive awareness."

We also found that Thorin had been separated from his class during the school year more than we were led to believe. During those times, he was working with the special education case manager, Mrs. Mallory.

"Why didn't we know that?" asked Ward.

The principal spoke up. "His IEP states 60 to 90 percent of the time in the regular classroom."

"I didn't remember such a wide margin," I said.

Turning to Mrs. Mallory, I asked, "What was he working on with you?"

"Various things."

The principal interrupted, "Why don't you meet privately with Mrs. Mallory and get those questions answered. She can also go over summer school options."

After the meeting, Ward and I talked in the car as we drove back to work.

"I can't keep up. It's too much information."

"I know," he said "But we're fine. We're figuring it out."

I needed to believe that against all reason. Reason was telling me the school might have a vested interest in Thorin being special. It could've been unconscious like Abraham Maslow's observation: "If you only have a hammer, you tend to see every problem as a nail." But what if they thought he was a problem?

The next week, I met with Mrs. Mallory.

"It must have been hard to hear Thorin can't attend regular summer school," she said sympathetically.

"It was hard to hear."

"Would it be nice to hear some options?"

"Yes."

She showed me a chart with the summer school options for special education students. She kept it close to her, so I wasn't able to read the words. In the first option, she told me the students didn't have any regular interaction with people outside the classroom. It sounded like the dungeon room in *Game of Thrones*; you're not sure how you got there, but clearly someone doesn't like you.

"We don't want him there do we?" she said as she patted my hand, smiling and shaking her head.

"No."

She ran her finger over the descriptions of the next three rooms, making thoughtful murmurings. Surely she'd seen this chart before this moment but she was acting like it had just been flown in by a three-eyed crow. Finally, she looked up at me.

"No! No! No!" she said dismissing them. "Not for him!"

I was relieved but I had no idea why. As she read the last description silently, her mouth broke in a wide smile. She tapped her finger excitedly on the paper, "This one has a lot of support!"

I shook my head, "Why can't he be in an inclusive classroom in the summer?"

"They won't give him an aide," she replied—"they" being the Tywin Lannister's in the district office.

"Um, I'm comfortable advocating for an aide."

"He won't have as much fun in the regular classroom."

Seriously? Other kids are in school to learn. The expectation for Thorin is not to mitigate the fun factor.

"Do they work on reading and writing there?" I asked. "Because he can't do those things yet."

"You know what you are? You're a pioneer!"

"What?"

"You're undertaking something that hasn't been done before."

"Inclusive summer school?" I guessed.

Mrs. Mallory's illogical cognitive leaps were exhausting me and caused me to forget to ask what she worked on with Thorin during the year. These people were so much better at excluding Thorin than Ward and I were at trying to get him included. But then again, they had 400 years of experience keeping kids like him out altogether.

The Individuals with Disabilities Education Act (IDEA), ratified by Congress in 1975, ensures that children with disabilities have the opportunity to receive a free, appropriate public education in the least restrictive environment, just like other children. How was what we were asking for considered radical in 2012? I couldn't believe anyone in our city or state had never asked for their child to be in an inclusive summer school classroom.

I tried finding another parent who had accomplished this near-Herculean task. I posted my question on the Facebook page of the local Down syndrome parents' group. No one who responded even mentioned summer school. Most of the comments came from families who lived in rural Maine, and their stories were worse. Parents shared that their school could not accommodate inclusion at any time during the year; others shared that their child was bused to a developmental classroom fifteen miles away from home and the school their siblings attended; and some were in legal battles with their school districts.

I called the office of our state university, which specialized in inclusion and disability. The adage "Those that can, do. Those who can't, teach" was apt in this case. I spoke with a professor there who was supportive, but I knew more about the school system and barriers to inclusion than he did.

With no evidence of inclusive summer school in Maine, I emailed the director of special services in our district, Joan Croft, hoping for at least a response. Eleven minutes later, I got back a four-paragraph email on the merits of inclusion! She also wrote that we should get together and talk. I was dizzy with glee.

The following week, I arrived for our meeting. I wanted to project myself as a calm and engaged parent; I wore a pencil skirt and sensible heels. She rounded the corner of the reception area as I came in. It was casual Friday; she had on jeans, a white T-shirt, and a tan blazer. I was impressed that she came to escort me to her office. During our conversation, I thanked her profusely for her commitment to inclusion.

"It doesn't make sense to support inclusion only nine months out of the year. It's backpedaling," she said.

"Exactly!"

"You contacted me at the right time. We just received a pilot project grant for kindergarten and first grade inclusion summer school."

"What? Oh, my gosh! I can't believe it!" Talk about your wildest dreams being answered.

She laughed good-naturedly then asked me, "Would you want Thorin to attend?"

"Yes!" I said. "We would like very much for him to attend."

She went on to explain how the class would operate.

"Because it is true inclusion, there will be a fifty-fifty ratio of students with and without disabilities. We will have co-teachers and an aide for support. Right now, it looks like eight or nine students. The students are coming from all over the city so everyone will be new."

What the director described was exactly what I had been reading about in books and had heard at a recent conference on inclusion.

"It sounds perfect! I have one more item. Thorin needs a communication device at school. He uses Proloquo2Go, which he loves. So much of the frustration is from him not being able to talk or be understood."

"Let's get him an iPad and the program! I'll have it at the summer program!"

I thought I was going to end up on the floor sobbing with true gratitude. We were finally on the right track!

———

Kindergarten came to a close. Despite the challenges, Thorin ended on a good note. Ms. Charles and Lo-Lo had been on his side. He clearly adored them both. Lo-Lo announced she was retiring. She told him, "I'm lucky you were my last student, Thorin."

Ms. Charles pulled both of us into the art room on the last day of school. A couple of teachers were putting the finishing touches on gifts for Lo-Lo's retirement party. They had matted and framed a painting made of the handprints of the students in Thorin's class. Their other creation was a pair of over-sized, yellow glasses for her to wear at the dinner. The eyeholes had capital Ls on both sides of the openings so it spelled out "Lo-Lo," the name Thorin bestowed on her. The glasses were yellow because it was Thorin's favorite color. Thorin and I both squealed and clapped.

Thorin wouldn't start summer school until July. He spent a lot of time with Bubba while Ward and I were at work. He would bring his iPad with him on his visits. The iPad also had a camera, which we didn't give much thought to.

When I got home one afternoon, my mom pulled me aside. She pushed the camera icon on the iPad screen and revealed a photo of Thorin—more accurately a selfie. The image was Thorin's bisected face peering into the lens of the camera; his hand was placed along his jaw with his fingers partially curled except for his pinky, which pointed toward the camera. The background was the top part of the kitchen door molding with a bit of the wall and ceiling.

I looked at my mom. "It's such a private moment."

She nodded, "There's more."

We moved from one image to another. In total, there were twenty-three selfies from that particular vantage point, but in each he did something a little different, showing more of his face, less of his face, or a different expression.

"These are good, right?" I asked.

"I think they are."

After we scrolled through the selfies, we found photos of a box of Life cereal, his favorite at the time.

"That's very Warhol!" I said, and we both laughed.

We told Thorin how much we enjoyed his photos.

"You like taking pictures?" I asked.

"Yesith! Yesith! Yesith!"

"Do you like . . ."

Thorin interrupted, "No. No. No."

"Thorin wants to take photos, but he doesn't want to talk about it," my mom offered.

A couple days later, Thorin took his iPad to a doctor's appointment. While I waited in the reception area, Ward went with him into the hall. Thorin took photos of stairs, hallways, windows, plants, furniture, and a skylight. None of his shots were straight on or centered, and he favored a right angle of partial images. We had gotten the iPad for Thorin to be able to communicate with the world, which he was doing through his photos.

As we were leaving for a walk a few days later, Thorin grabbed his iPad. I noticed he would take a photo then view it and reshoot, if necessary. He might do that three or four times until he was satisfied. On that walk, he took some little portrait shots of the dogs and one of Ward and me. The rest were more documentary images, such as trees and electrical poles bisected horizontally by a train moving through the scene or a car bisected vertically by an electrical pole.

There was a beautiful shot of Ward walking from behind framed by electrical wires, the street, and curb.

Thorin was showing his photos to other people and enjoying the praise he got. He did not want to be asked to take photos. He had no interest in someone picking the subject to be photographed. It was clear Thorin had his own ideas and vision.

Even though Thorin enjoyed spending time with Bubba, summer school soon arrived. The school was in our old neighborhood, and Thorin had been at the playground countless times—both Ella and Evvy attended school there. When we walked in, there was general confusion with multiple programs starting at the same time as well as specific confusion about where his aide was.

Thorin and I stood in the reception area waiting for her. I wanted him to meet his aide before he got in the classroom. She arrived late, complaining the rain had made her trip from the suburbs longer than anticipated. She was in her fifties and wore a red slash of lipstick, a black turtleneck dress, and a belted trench coat. Instead of offering her name, she said, "My hair is a disaster!" I waited for her to sort herself out before I introduced Thorin and myself. When she finally looked at Thorin, she blanched. I instantly despised her.

Smoothing her hair she said, "I haven't worked in years. I was a social worker. I've never worked with a . . ."

I decided to help her out for Thorin's sake. "With such a young person? Is that what you were going to say?"

"Sure."

I insisted on walking him to the classroom with her. I was shocked by the size of the other children. I realized Thorin was quite small, yet they looked like giants. When I finally got the teacher's attention, I made introductions.

"Oh, hello! Excuse the first day chaos," she responded.

"No prob. These kids are all in kindergarten or first grade?"

"No. They're in second to fourth grade."

I had a sinking feeling. "Where's the inclusive classroom with the younger children?"

"I don't know."

I told Thorin we would have to go back downstairs. As we were leaving, a woman introduced herself to Thorin and me. She was from the special services department at the district.

"I wanted to make sure everything went well today."

"Oh, thank you! I was just going downstairs to find out where the inclusive summer program meets."

"Not necessary. This is Thorin's classroom."

"He's six. He hasn't been in first grade yet."

"Don't worry."

I should have left with Thorin but I didn't. I thought—as Tim Gunn had advised *Project Runway* designers for years—we could make it work. Also the act of leaving school was counterintuitive. Where would Thorin go?

When I came back a few hours later to pick up Thorin, I found out that none of the students did much of anything. Whatever this program was, it had been slapped together starting that day. I also found out that all the students in Thorin's class knew each other because they attended the school year round. I was relieved to know Thorin's speech therapist and occupational therapist from kindergarten were visiting almost every day to work with him.

The second day was somewhat better, but the teacher seemed overwhelmed, which I could understand. She had no time to plan for the session, hitting the ground running the day before. Thorin's aide—whom I had privately christened Mrs. John Updike because of her 1960s mentality, her narcissistic ways, and the fact she was a boob—told me Thorin refused to go back to class following break. After twenty minutes, the speech therapist intervened and told him to get back to class, which he did. Mrs. Updike then told me that she was "hoping to get some magic words from the speech therapist," so he would listen to her. I was hoping for some magic words to turn her into a toad.

It wasn't like Thorin not to go back in to the classroom. A witness to the event told me Mrs. Updike was literally pulling at her hair in frustration. I knew Thorin would find that irresistible. The program was four weeks long; it had to get better quickly. I emailed Joan Croft, who I thought was my inclusion maven.

We are not happy with the summer program Thorin is in. It seems very unorganized. The children are grades older than Thorin, and it's not inclusive. His aide is not up to the task. We need to get to the bottom of this soon. We look forward to hearing from you.

She wrote back. Ward and I read her email together.

I understand your frustration, and we will work to make sure that Thorin is appropriately supported in the program. This program is a "regular education" initiative, not a special education program. As you know, Thorin was scheduled to be in a special education, self-contained program for summer. Then, we received the grant! This is only the third day of services. I will be sending over a teacher consultant to help the teacher and aide. Let's give it some more time.

I turned to Ward and asked, "Does that mean she has no control over the program?"

Ward responded with another question. "Why wouldn't the special education department be part of the administration of an inclusive program?"

"Something is off."

"I agree. It's like the inclusion piece is a secret. But from whom? The education department, the teacher, or us?"

Ward took Thorin to school the next day. Mrs. Updike was less than thrilled when she saw Thorin.

"I thought maybe he wasn't coming back."

Ward asked Thorin, "Hey, Dude. Can you go to the library while I talk with your aide?" Thorin was out of earshot before he turned to Mrs. Updike and said, "What's the problem?"

"I don't know how to work with a Down syndrome person."

"A person with Down syndrome."

"That's what I said."

"No you didn't. He's a child who has Down syndrome. He's not Down syndrome."

"They're sending a consultant for you and the teacher. That should help Thorin," Ward said, not hiding his disgust.

When I picked up Thorin, he ran from me through the open theater door on the other side of the hallway. He sat on the stage.

"What are you doing?"

"No."

"You don't want to tell me?"

"No."

I went up to him and said, politely, "Please come with me."

He stood up and pressed himself against the back wall. I knelt down. I went to pull him toward me. He brought his arm down on my head so hard my glasses fell off.

"Thorin! What's happening?" I asked, shaking.

This was not Thorin. I fought back tears. Eventually, he let me lead him outside and told me he didn't want to go back to school.

"Thorin, I'm sorry. I am. Daddy and I can fix this."

"No!"

"A woman is coming to help, okay?"

He didn't respond, but his day did get better; we went to see Bubba. Ward and I talked it over when we got home.

"I understand he's frustrated, but he doesn't get to call the shots."

"Right, but this isn't the program we were promised. It's a shit show there," I said.

"Kari, I don't think we have an alternative. Do we?"

"No."

What neither of us could acknowledge was that Thorin was changing. He had never hit anyone like that. Behavior is communication. What was he trying to tell us?

———

It wasn't just the staff that was the problem. The next day, I talked to some kids at the school about staring, pointing, and making funny faces at Thorin. I also notified his teacher.

"Well no one knows him so they're curious," she said smiling weakly.

I was furious. "Those gestures don't indicate curiosity."

"I don't know what else it could be."

Was I bumping up against her ingrained sense of deniability? The school had colorful posters stating it was a bully-free zone. I guess if staff members play ignorant to actions constituting bullying then, voilà, you have a bully-free zone!

I met the teacher consultant, Marie, the following day. She seemed to be getting herself up to speed quickly. She told me she had read Thorin's school records and had already talked to his aide, Mrs. Updike.

Referring to Mrs. Updike she explained, "I can try to educate her but . . ."

"Okay, I get it."

"I'm going to his regular school to get some more information. I'll fill you in."

She called me later that day. "Did you know they have two kindergarten and first grade summer classes going on there? There's six or seven students in each."

"I knew there was one with some kids from his kindergarten class."

"Why wasn't he placed there?"

I gave her the details.

"That's where he should have been," she said. "It's perfect for him—his school, students he knows, small class size."

Before I contacted Joan Croft and Thorin's principal, I called the school district's grant manager. I told her what program we had been promised, including the name of the foundation funding the project, all according to Joan Croft. I could hear the strain in her voice.

"We did get a grant from that foundation, but it isn't for the program you described. I'm not aware of that program."

"They just stuck him in that classroom without planning, preparation, or supports! That's not right," I told her.

"I'm sorry. I don't have anything to do with that."

It was so hard to believe we had been lied to. I couldn't compute it. I felt stalled.

When I went to get Thorin, I was told he refused to go into his classroom. Between Marie, the speech therapist, and occupational therapist, they figured out his day for him, away from class. We requested Thorin be moved to his regular school. We were told he would not have an aide because Mrs. Updike needed to stay where she was. We didn't want her anyway—a trained monkey would have exhibited more grace and skill. In a desperate move, I emailed Ms. Charles to tell her what was going on. My subject heading read "PLEASE HELP ME."

A few hours later, she emailed with her phone number. When we talked, she explained she would co-teach one of the summer school classes, so Thorin would have enough support to participate. Her focus would be for Thorin to learn—and to love school again. She gave up two weeks of her summer break to do this for him. The tears started, and I could barely get out my thanks.

"I wouldn't do this for anyone, but it's Thorin."

"You get him," I said crying.

"I do."

I told Thorin about going back to his school and working with Ms. Charles.

"Good!" he said.

"Are you excited to go back with her?"

"Yesith!"

When I dropped Thorin off with Ms. Charles, she and I both had tears in our eyes. Thorin ran for a hug. He was back in good hands. Ward and I were still furious Thorin had been placed in such a destructive environment.

"Inclusion is not a sink or swim situation! They have to believe it's an important model. They have to support it," I told Ward.

"Thorin shouldn't have the obligation to be included. This treatment of him—like he is the problem—stops. Kari, we're in over our heads."

"Yesith!" My response gave us both a much-needed laugh.

Ward decided to send an email to the superintendent of schools in our district and our school board members to apprise them of the summer events. Our superintendent was relatively new to our city and the position.

> *Dear Superintendent Samuel,*
> *Welcome to Portland. I hope your tenure here is filled with positive experiences and personal triumphs. This isn't one of them. I am writing to you and our school board members to register my family's extreme displeasure with the shabby treatment of our son, Thorin, throughout the recent failed attempt to integrate him into a summer school class.*

Ward went on to enumerate the challenges since April when the principal said Thorin couldn't attend inclusive summer school. The responses from the superintendent and the board members, who responded, were diplomatic. They offered thanks for being notified and gratitude for the resolution of the problem for Thorin. There was no acknowledgment in any of their responses that they were troubled that the director of special services had lied about an inclusive classroom or that Thorin's aide was hostile to working with a child who had Down syndrome.

Ms. Charles was true to her word. She worked with Thorin on reading and loving school. She suggested we get copies of the books she used. She also made arrangements for Thorin and me to meet his first grade teacher, Mrs. Bruce. On the last day of class, the four of us met in the cafeteria. After introductions, she asked Thorin to take Mrs. Bruce's photo for his iPad.

Turning to Mrs. Bruce she said, "See, he uses this to communicate! It's awesome. He'll put your photo in here, then we'll label it with your name."

Mrs. Bruce had a blank expression on her face, but she did stand patiently while Thorin took her photo. Ms. Charles and Thorin then huddled at one of the tables to upload the photo. As I watched them, I was struck by how well they worked together.

"Thorin, I'm all thumbs! Help me!" Ms. Charles said.

He laughed and leaned in to see what she had done. They figured it out then proudly showed Mrs. Bruce. She gave a tepid response, but I decided not to judge her by that. Ms. Charles was a firecracker, and most people looked tepid compared to her.

―――

My mom found another set of selfies on Thorin's iPad. We figured out from the photos he was in the spare bedroom at Aunt Betty and Uncle Matt's apartment. Thorin had changed the photo setting so his photos had a Warhol-like silkscreen effect. All the photos were bathed in neon green, florescent yellow, electric blue, and tomato soup red with Thorin in various poses: sticking out his tongue; making more funny faces; showing half his face and his arm above his head; raising an eyebrow; and zooming in on one eye with an elbow over his head. Also, there were some photos of Uncle Matt working at his desk in the room.

"Did you know Thorin was taking photos during his visit?" I asked my sister.

"No," she said, "but he did say he was working."

―――

Before school started in the fall, I ran into someone from the school district at the grocery store. The person shared with me that the whole summer experience was disturbing and wrong and counseled us to retain a professional disability advocate. If we were interested, this person would set up a meeting with an advocate on our behalf. I called Ward and explained the brief conversation.

"We have a Deep Throat on our side!" I told him.

"We're doing it! Set it up!"

I met the advocate, Trisha, at a playground. She wore an oversize T-shirt with built-in shoulder pads and black slacks. I brought Thorin, and she brought her two children. While they played, we talked. Her first order of business was her appraisal of Joan Croft, the special services director.

"She's a liar! She's lied to all my clients. You said you wanted an inclusive classroom for Thorin, so she made one up! If you said Thorin needed a pony, she'd say they just bought a horse farm. Got it? She will say anything to get you off her case."

As we continued talking, I remembered something that didn't seem important before, but listening to Trisha made me think of it differently. Trisha must have noticed a change in my demeanor.

"What's going on?" she inquired.

"Joan Croft was insistent Thorin take the bus to the other school. I insisted on driving him."

"Well, you probably wouldn't have caught on as fast if he took the bus. It isn't like he could tell you," Trisha said and then went on to her next thought. "And forget Superintendent Samuel; he's gone in another year or so. He took this job to have the title of superintendent on his resume. He wants to be in a big city. He's marking time."

Trisha sounded angry and knowledgeable about the scene. I wondered if Ward and my naiveté about all things school had made things worse for Thorin. Angry and knowledgeable sounded about right.

Our main concerns for first grade were for Thorin to have a communication device in the classroom and a proper aide. At home, Thorin was using the iPad for communicating if he got stuck, and we wanted him to use it at school. I talked to the principal and told her one of his substitute aides from the previous year knew the program and was looking for a position. She informed me it didn't work that way, and Thorin would get who was available. When I told Trisha what happened, she told us to get a device included in his IEP. She also wrote up a list of parental concerns for us to submit.

Joan Croft was included on the request for a communication device. She offered to bring in a speech and language consultant to assess what device Thorin needed. Hadn't Thorin made that assessment with his preference for Proloquo2Go for the last several months? I offered that he could bring his iPad but was told the school didn't want to be responsible for it.

Two days before the start of first grade, we didn't have a communication device for Thorin and didn't know who his aide would be. I talked to the principal.

"School starts in two days. You don't have any idea who you will assign."

"Not yet."

"Will you know tomorrow?"

"Yes."

"Can Thorin come in to meet her?"

"No, she'll be busy."

"Can Thorin come in to meet her before class on the first day? Even ten minutes would make a huge difference with all the stimulation of a new class, teacher, and aide. It's a lot for Thorin to process."

"She won't start until 8:55 A.M. We don't start paying her until then."

I knew that was bullshit. "Class starts at 8:50 A.M. He will meet her in class, in front of everyone, five minutes after class begins?" I said sharply.

"Yes."

It was punitive. Why take it out on Thorin? I wanted to ask her if we could be real and talk to each other like human beings for three minutes, but clearly she couldn't do that.

Ward and I decided I would walk Thorin to the classroom on the first day. Mrs. Mallory said I couldn't go in, so I told Thorin goodbye at the door.

"Have fun," I said weakly.

Thorin walked in to the classroom, sat at a desk in the front row, and put his head down; I watched him from behind a pillar in the hall, so he couldn't see me. It was so different from Ms. Charles the previous year. A few minutes later, I saw Miss Jane, his new Ed Tech, who was wearing pedal pushers and a polo shirt with anklet socks and sneakers. She walked over to Thorin and tapped him gently on the shoulder. He looked up and smiled. I saw her say something and put her hand out. They shook hands. So far, so good! Mrs. Mallory sidled up to me behind the pillar. Before she had a chance to say anything, I told her, "I'm not leaving this spot."

I saw Thorin sit upright, turning his attention to the front of the class. Instead of sitting down, she stood next to his desk, hovering. And then, she did something that might not have been noticed by anyone else. Smiling she reached down, interrupting his focus on the teacher, and made a small tap on the tip of his nose. He was in first grade and a month from being seven years old. One of his biggest fears was being treated like a baby.

Later that day, Thorin brought home a sheet of paper, a letter written to Ward and me. The note was brief: "Dear Mommy and Daddy, I love you both."

After reading it over, I asked Thorin, "Who wrote this?"

"Her," he said angrily.

"The aide?"

"Yesith."

"Did you tell her what to write?"

"No!"

In my head, I was thinking some fifty-five-year-old lady just wrote us a mash note.

"Are you okay with that? Do you want her to write for you?"

"No!"

"Okay, me either. Let's tell her tomorrow."

"Good!"

The next morning, I told Mrs. Mallory that Thorin and I wanted to talk with Miss Jane—as I had come to think of her—about writing his assignments.

"Let's get a little group together to talk. I want to add the speech therapist, and I should be there, too," she said.

The number of attendees seemed like overkill. I had wanted to handle the manner swiftly; however, I agreed. Once we all sat down, I quickly explained that Thorin and I didn't want her writing his work.

Miss Jane tried to speak, but she was cut off by the speech therapist, "Is that true, Thorin?"

Thorin looked at me. I shook my head and said, "I don't understand."

"How did Thorin tell you that?" she asked.

I immediately felt of a sense of déjà vu. "It was in a conversation."

"How did he say it?"

Why was she casting suspicion on Thorin's abilities? Was it so impossible for her to believe Thorin might have an opinion? I couldn't possibly hope to tackle that conversation in front of Thorin given her attitude.

"Here's the deal," I said, "Miss Jane should not write for Thorin. She should help him write by himself."

Mrs. Mallory wrapped up the meeting with promises no one would write for Thorin.

A few hours later, I received a call from the school that Thorin had vomited and soiled his pants. I picked him up from the nurse, who had given him a change of clothing. In the car, Thorin told me, "No more school," which made me want to vomit.

Mrs. Bruce, his teacher, emailed to see how he was doing and said the other children were worried about him. Ward and I kept him home from school the next day. We were both hoping it was a flu bug and not something to do with school. Yes, that seemed ridiculous, then and more so now, but we wanted to project that school was fine—there didn't seem to be any other choice.

When Thorin returned to school, he was assigned a new special education case manager; Mrs. Mallory had been reassigned by the principal. The new case manager was named Mrs. Dean. We received no explanation for the switch.

A couple of days later, I had to pick up Thorin early for an appointment with the pulmonologist; his asthma was acting up. When we left the main office, he told me he had to poop. I waited for him in the hallway outside the boy's room. As fate would have it, Miss Jane was walking to the office.

"Where's Thorin?"

I motioned to the bathroom.

Shaking her head, she said, "I wouldn't leave him in there alone. He could lock the stall."

"He should lock the stall," I replied, correcting her.

"He locked the stall the other day and wouldn't come out."

I gritted my teeth, "Well, he must have come out eventually."

"I don't let him use public bathrooms anymore. He has to use the private ones, and I wedge my shoe in the doorway so he can't lock it."

"What? So, he never gets a chance to do it right, again? That's not a solution."

Still shaking her head, she said in a cloying tone, "You really have a time of it, don't you?"

"Yeah, I don't know about that." I was silently sending what I hope were telepathic messages to Thorin to hurry it up.

"He ran away from me."

"Who wouldn't, you fucking jerk!" I wanted to scream. Instead, I settled for an "Uh huh."

"He hid in a locker. It took forever to find him."

"That's an exaggeration," using my most snarky voice.

I turned away from her while I continued to wait for Thorin. If I had seen a locker big enough, I would have jumped in it.

Later in the day, I emailed both her and Mrs. Dean.

Hello. Following up on a brief conversation I had with Miss Jane today. Apparently one day, Thorin refused to unlock the bathroom stall for a period of time. Since then he isn't allowed to use a public restroom, and the bathroom he uses is not allowed to be locked. I think, Miss Jane, you said you put your foot in the door? I think a kid testing the limits is "typical behavior." Not allowing him privacy ever again, never allows him to do it right. We are

*requesting Thorin be allowed privacy in the bathroom like any
other student.*

*Tip: Don't make a big deal out of it, and he won't have a show
to put on for anyone. Thank you.*

Mrs. Dean emailed back offering to create a laminated series of
cards with the steps of appropriate bathroom behavior for Thorin.
Why did she think the problem person in my email was Thorin? I
also knew Thorin would have a field day with those cards. And some
part of me wanted to agree, only to see what the cards would look
like, but I went to the principal instead. I was shocked because she
agreed with me. She told both Miss Jane and Mrs. Dean that Thorin
deserved privacy and to stop making it an issue.

I didn't trust Miss Jane to make on-the-spot decisions in Thorin's
best interest because her instinct was to infantilize him. Ward and I
didn't believe in taming Thorin's development by physical control.
Similar to any child, Thorin put us through the paces: running in
the street, hiding in the clothing racks at Target, throwing objects,
leaving the house without our knowledge, hiding my keys, etc. The
list was extensive—no different from other children.

We had been lucky to have Sherry, Thorin's foster-mother, as
our parent coach. One of the best suggestions that she gave me
was not to control Thorin, instead teach him self-control. She told
me about a former foster child who was a six-year-old girl. Sherry's
home was her third placement, and the girl was known to be a
"runner." When she ran for the first time, Sherry shouted after
her, "If you see a bear, stop running!" The girl turned around and
went back in the house. I told Sherry if she ever wrote a book
about her exploits as a foster mother she should use that advice as
the title.

Sherry also told me something that is probably at the heart of parenting: "Parents, especially now, don't know they can ignore most things. They over-parent. The kid feels overwhelmed, and the parent is tired. What a waste of time."

———

In September, we attended an IEP meeting for the annual review of Thorin's goals. His teacher, Mrs. Bruce, was asked to report first.

"He's physically aggressive," she said, sounding scripted and rehearsed.

That didn't seem like a very nice—or accurate—thing to say about anyone, let alone one of your students. "Exactly how was he aggressive?" I said, seething.

Trisha, our advocate, kicked me hard under the table. *Talk about physically aggressive.* Then, Ward patted my hand. They were so good cop, bad cop.

"He pushes and pokes the other children," she explained.

Are you serious?

We had never received the occupational therapist's report on proprioceptive awareness because she was assigned to a different school. I looked to Thorin's new occupational therapist; it seemed they only listened to each other, not Ward or me.

"Your colleague described that as proprioceptive awareness."

She smiled. "Okay."

To Mrs. Dean's credit, she said, "I don't think we should label Thorin's behavior as physically aggressive. He's not aggressive."

The occupational therapist smiled again and said, "Okay."

I couldn't stomach any of them. The truth appeared to be a moving target. And, I was the mother bear who was inept at defending her young. Every move led Thorin further into a trap, a snare.

After the meeting, I emailed Trisha and told her I wanted to homeschool. I had no idea how we could actually do that and I hadn't even said anything to Ward. I had to get Thorin out of there. She emailed back.

> *Homeschooling is not a great option now. Laws are changing about homeschooling and related services, which could mean Thorin would not get any services from the district. It would be all out of pocket. We have to get through the evaluations first. We can fix this.*

I didn't mention my email or response from Trisha to Ward and hoped we could fix this.

The following week, the school nurse called to say Thorin had wet himself. I went to the school.

"He never goes when I go with him. Then, he wets himself," Miss Jane informed me.

"What do you mean, when you go with him?"

"I stand outside the door."

"No, do not do that," my frustration evident. "Has it occurred to you he isn't comfortable going to the bathroom with you right outside the door?"

WTF! Hadn't we already gone over this? Leave him the fuck alone in the bathroom!

"What do you want me to do?"

I wanted to scream, "Be better at your job!" Instead, I told her I had to think this through, which became my new comeback to the worst ideas offered. I needed something that could address the systematic focus of infantilizing Thorin rather than running around to put out the same fire.

It was clear Miss Jane saw her job as controlling Thorin's behavior more so than helping him learn reading, writing, and math.

After conferring with Ward, I asked to have Miss Jane removed as his aide. I also requested, again, that Thorin be given privacy in the bathroom.

The principal complied with my requests. Thorin's new aide reminded me of a drill sergeant in a blue jean jumper. On her first day, I had a quick conversation with her after Thorin went into the classroom.

"I know you're tough."

"I am tough but fair. I think Thorin is capable."

Her response was something I hadn't heard before.

"So do I. Thank you."

Thorin wet himself three days in a row, and I left a message for The Pee Whisper. Sarge, as I thought of Thorin's new aide, suggested maybe she should pretend not to notice his wet pants, then he would have to wear them. She believed the discomfort would probably make him stop doing it. The fact that she didn't think Thorin would bring up having wet pants was mind-boggling, so I went to my standby comment: "I have to think about that."

I ran to the car to call The Pee Whisperer's office again, saying it was critical. She called twenty minutes later.

"He cannot be punished in any way," she relayed.

"I know!"

"Is he doing this at home?"

"No."

"I'm comfortable calling it situational anxiety related to school. Regression is normal in times of stress. I'm going to give you a protocol for the staff to follow. Get it out to them today. It's four steps. Easy! Tell someone to call me with questions."

I wrote the instructions using bullet points and explained they were from a professional social worker at a pediatric behavioral clinic. I included her name and phone number and emailed it to Mrs. Dean. The next morning, I met with Mrs. Dean, Mrs. Bruce, and the occupational therapist to go over the protocol. Sarge was not there, but Mrs. Dean and Mrs. Bruce promised a copy would be provided to her that day.

Two days later at 3:10 P.M., Ward got a phone call at work from a staff person at the after-school recreation program. Sarge had accompanied Thorin to the recreation program in the cafeteria a few minutes earlier. In front of Thorin and other children, she told the recreation staff, "We're in a power struggle. He wet his pants and wants dry ones. Do not give him dry clothes." She then left.

Ward headed to the school with a set of dry clothes. Thorin came home with him, crying. That night he peed in his bed. I thought I was going to have a stroke, and, for the first time, I brought up homeschooling to Ward.

"Kari, I don't want to discuss that. I want to move forward."

"We can't let Thorin continue. The problem is systemic. This is how the districts deals with a child who has Down syndrome."

"I want to focus on addressing what happened. We decided this path was important. They are required to figure it out."

We kept Thorin home until we decided what to do next. Bubba came to the rescue to babysit.

"Thorin little baby," he told her.

"Thorin you are not. You are a big boy! Your Bubba's big boy."

Hanging out with Bubba, watching movies, and reading was the best recovery program, ever, for Thorin.

—————

We tried resolving things at the school level by requesting an emergency IEP meeting. Prior to the meeting, we sent documentation, which included an incident report we had requested from the city's recreation staff—stating what had transpired with the additional information that Sarge had said not to notify Thorin's parents—and the school's daily communication log that had been sent in Thorin's backpack that day. The log was a record of Thorin's school day, recorded by Sarge.

> *(On the front of the log)*
> 2:15 P.M.: Bathroom ☹
> 2:30 P.M.: Classroom: "Work refusal"
> 2:50 P.M.: School released
> *(On the back of the log)*
> Bathroom: 2:15–2:30 P.M. Peed on his pants. I did not stay in the bathroom but stood outside with the door ajar. Checked every five minutes.

At the IEP meeting, Joan Croft said, "What occurred was a communication misunderstanding. The aide had been acting on instructions that had come directly from the mother."

I came out of my seat and yelled, "That's a lie!"

Joan Croft countered, "We are not going to discuss this any further. We will move on."

As I stood hunched over at the table, time was suspended. Ward put his hand on my back, guiding me back in my seat. The die had been cast; Thorin had a terrible mother—she has a time of it, you know. They had ignored all the documentation we provided. Sarge had told the recreation staff not to notify us. Why would she do that if she was acting on my instructions?

We escalated to the next level and filed a formal complaint with the school district. We received a terse letter from the human resources department, which stated they had done its own investigation. Investigators interviewed Sarge as well as the principal and Joan Croft, both of whom were not in the building at the time of the incident; they did not speak to the staff at the recreation program. We were notified that if there were any disciplinary action, we would not be appraised. In addition, we had to request that Sarge be replaced as Thorin's aide.

We were traveling through another dimension, a dimension not only of sight and sound but of incompetence, deceit, and judgment. Our journey took us away from a wondrous land whose boundaries included everyone.

Thorin dressed as Thor

CHAPTER SEVEN

The Littlest Avenger

I contacted scores of parents with children who had Down syndrome or cognitive disabilities in our state, and beyond, through social media. Many were in our shoes, or more aptly, their children were in Thorin's shoes. I read articles by professionals and parents regarding children in self-contained and inclusive classrooms; criticism was aimed at the implementation of both models.

Some families had also thought of homeschooling or were already homeschooling. One of the biggest stumbling blocks to leaving school was the belief the school system won if it never had to figure out how to inclusively educate children with disabilities, particularly those who were neurologically different from the norm. Additionally, most parents could not financially afford the homeschool option.

I contacted All Born (in), a sister site of the Northwest Down Syndrome Association in Portland, Oregon. The parent-driven organization helps educate parents on best practices for working with their school districts on inclusion. The woman I spoke to admitted it can be an uphill battle since inclusion was a foreign concept to most districts. She also shared something else with me: "The federal protection on what a least restrictive environment is for students with disabilities is not defined. It's hard to enforce something when no one agrees on what it is."

After several conversations, Ward and I also didn't believe we could financially afford to homeschool. Our focus turned to how to keep Thorin engaged and learning at school.

Thorin was assigned two Ed Techs when he returned to school. Mrs. Shelby worked with him in the morning, and Ms. Alice assisted in the afternoon. Both women were friendly and spoke positively about him. Ms. Alice was working on a master's degree in special education.

During Thorin's time away from school, we visited a local apple orchard. Thorin took dozens of photos with his iPad while we were there. His photos had a documentary feel with people captured during unguarded moments, not posed ones. Thorin was a boy who wasn't understood when he talked, but looking at his photos, one would assume a discerning eye took them. Not only was he was telling us about what he saw but also what he felt.

I asked Thorin if we could show the art teacher his photographs. He agreed. I was surprised Thorin wasn't shy or nervous when we went to see her. She nodded as she looked at the first one and then leaned in, examining each photograph carefully. Her face changed from polite interest to wonder.

"Thorin!" she said, looking at him, "These are really good!"

Thorin went up on his toes, putting his arms in the air. "Tanks!"

"Thorin, you're a good photographer. I love them!"

"Tanks!"

"And, they aren't great just for a seven-year-old; they're great for a person any age."

"They are great!" I couldn't contain my enthusiasm.

Thorin shot me a look signaling this was between the two of them.

"I have an empty case in the front hallway. These should go in there. What do you think, Thorin?"

"Yesith!"

The look on Thorin's face was sublime. I wished all his school experiences could be like this. He went off to class, and I stayed behind with the art teacher to chat a little more.

"These are great and not just for a boy with Down syndrome," she said. "He's got an eye. I think his photographs could change how people think about children with Down syndrome."

I took a step back. That shocked me. I believed it but I didn't expect her to say it. We had another ally!

That weekend, we printed the photographs, and Ward helped Thorin mount each photo on a thin board. What we didn't know was that Ward had bought small, wire easels for each of the photographs.

"Thorin, your photographs can go on these," he said as he moved a photograph onto one of them.

"Wow! Like a real artist!" I said.

"Daddy! Tanks!"

That Monday, the art teacher and Thorin decided where each photo should go in the glass display case. She handed a small sign to Thorin to place in front of his photographs: *Photographs by Thorin, 1st Grade.* When it was all set, the art teacher, Thorin, and I stood in front of the exhibit case in the main hall of the school, taking in the deliciously satisfying moment. It was what Thorin had longed for and what Ward and I had wanted for him. The moment was possible simply because the art teacher didn't see him as a problem to solve. She saw Thorin as someone worthy of contributing.

Thorin got a lot of praise for his photographs from students and staff. There were a few outliers who suggested Thorin was too incompetent to take the photographs, like the parent who asked me, "Does he know he's taking pictures?"

———

Thorin was still pushing and poking other children and touching their things—at least that's what we were told by Mrs. Dean. At this point, I was convinced it was a game to get Thorin in trouble. It sounded like the universal tattle, "He's touching me!"

One of the best things I learned from my dad about child rearing was "Nobody likes a rat." He never doled out a consequence based on tattling. He knew kids say things that are true and not so true to get attention. I shared my dad's wisdom with Ward, and he was not comfortable with me sharing it with the school. I suggested we have Trisha, our inclusion advocate, settle the debate. She had a whole other take on it.

"We should request a functional behavioral assessment be done on Thorin."

This was the last thing I wanted to hear, another person brought in to help Thorin.

"Trisha, Thorin is the recipient of the worst behavior. The Ed Techs told me they have to stop kids from picking him up, patting him on the head, and telling him what to do. We want the focus off Thorin."

"The behaviorist will work on the whole class. This dynamic can be revealed for what it is," she countered.

Including Thorin was an all-consuming task, and we hadn't even gotten to the education piece. Ward and I shared the same instinct for moving forward without a behaviorist, but we also weren't entirely sure we knew what we were doing. We were paying Trisha to help us, so we decided to listen to her.

Ward and I also decided another IEP meeting was in order. There were so many moving parts; it was hard to know what was happening. I approached Mrs. Dean and Joan Croft about an IEP meeting to discuss the implementation of a much-needed communication device, the behavioral concerns, and educational goals. The meeting was set for a month away. In the meantime, Joan Croft suggested we move to our assigned neighborhood school, old Walt Whitman High, where they wanted to place Thorin in a self-contained classroom. Mrs. Dean suggested we homeschool Thorin. It was that moment when you know you and your kid were no longer welcomed.

I even got into an argument with my mom about Thorin's schooling. She thought what we were doing was unfair to Thorin and suggested we try the self-contained classroom. I tried explaining.

"There's no guarantee he will learn there either."

"Well what about David? He doesn't have problems."

David was the only other child at the school who had Down syndrome and had been at Thorin's preschool. My mom wasn't the only person to draw comparisons between Thorin and David. David was a year older and several inches taller than Thorin. He had dark hair, dark eyes, glasses, and his verbal communication skills were superior to Thorin's. When someone wasn't mistaking them for each other—which seemed very "they all look alike" to me—then they were comparing Thorin to David.

"They're two different people. Besides, David is in an inclusive classroom."

"Maybe Thorin shouldn't be."

"Well it's what we're doing."

I realized the difficulties at school were a reflection of what people in general think about a child with Down syndrome: They are not like the rest of us. Worse, they are less than us. And, I wasn't just thinking about it; I was writing about it on the blog. The blog became my connection to other families who were struggling. I found it isolating to figure out what was best for Thorin. Sharing what was happening on my blog made it less lonely.

———

I had made a discovery! Albeit, it was a year before. One of my favorite authors, Chuck Klosterman, made fun of people with cognitive challenges. I had googled him out of curiosity when his appointment as the Ethicist at the *New York Times* was announced in 2012. While I was searching, I came upon a quote by Klosterman that floored me: "You used to be able to tell the difference between hipsters and homeless people. Now, it's between hipsters and retards. I mean, either that guy in the corner in orange safety pants holding a protest sign and wearing a top hat is mentally disabled or he is the coolest fucking guy you will ever know." I could not believe the writer I loved said that. Then, I discovered he had, at a book reading. Next, I searched "Chuck Klosterman and retarded" and found more examples. In his book *Fargo Rock City*, he wrote that he didn't want to sound insensitive yet continued to say ". . . show me a person whose intelligence equates to that of a dolphin and I will show you a fucking retard."

My next step was to search online for some instance where he had been chastised or called out for that usage. I couldn't find anything. How had a person who was deemed the Ethicist by the *New York Times* not been challenged on that ethical point? I felt like Melanie Griffith in the film *Working Girl*! In the same way Griffith had put together seemingly unrelated facts culled from newspapers and magazines to suggest a brilliant business acquisition, I had figured out that the *New*

York Times' Ethicist wasn't completely ethical. I had to do something! But, I didn't do anything for over a year. I had no idea how to go about addressing him.

I didn't tell anyone my discovery. Then, three things collided: I was gaining readers and a little reputation for what I was writing; Chuck Klosterman had recently published a new book *I Wear the Black Hat*; and I knew the problems Thorin faced at school were a reflection of systematic oppression directed at people with disabilities.

I finally told Ward what I discovered.

"Oh, no. Kari, do you really want to go down that road? We have enough going on."

"Hell, yes! We're losing this battle at the school because it's a bigger battle. It's out there! I want to change out there!"

"Settle down. What are you proposing?"

"I'm going to write him an open letter on the blog. I'll get others to share it!" Even as I said it, I knew it sounded like "I'll put on a show in my parents' garage!"

"How will you get people to share it?"

"I can do it! I know I can!"

I had never considered that part of my parenting duties would include activism but I knew I had to do something. The blog had become an extension of my parenting as an advocate; confronting Klosterman was too. I wrote my letter. It was short and to the point. Ward looked at it.

"Are you worried about what will happen?"

"I'm more worried what will happen if I don't. I'm doing it!"

For the first time in months, I felt like good things were possible for Thorin. With excitement and nervousness, I hit publish.

Was it a viral sensation? Well, I did get enough people to share my post that I was able to get Chuck Klosterman's attention—he sent me an email apologizing and offered to make a donation of $25,000 to an organization of my choosing. Also, I had permission to print his letter on my blog. I was interviewed on our local NBC affiliate, and *USA Today* picked up my story. It had worked!

He and I both did something unique. I had crafted a persuasive argument I knew would be hard to resist because he was, after all, the Ethicist—he would be a pretty crappy one if he didn't—and because he had just published a new book. No one wants bad press. As for Chuck Klosterman, no notable person to that point had so eloquently owned up to the mistake of using the R-word, and none had applied a self-imposed penalty of money. It was the icing on the cake.

My campaign resonated with many thousands of people who also knew the pain that word caused. I received hundreds of comments and emails. An email that best summed up what other parents communicated was by a father of a son who has Down syndrome: "I broke down in tears reading Mr. Klosterman's letter and I'm not a crier. I feel the world is better today for my son."

Not all parents have the additional charge of activism as part of their parenting duties. But for parents whose children are atypical, it can be a calling to make the world better for more than their child. Ellen Seidman, a popular disability writer and the author of the blog *Love That Max,* interviewed me about what had transpired. She asked me what I thought Thorin's reaction would be when he was old enough to read about it.

"Seriously, I hope it's something like, 'What else would I expect from you? You're my mother.' This is mother's work. This is my real job. Your kids aren't supposed to throw a parade every time you have their back."

When I found out I was going to be on the local news, I had a new concern. We never told Thorin he had Down syndrome. The subject had come up, but we weren't sure how knowing about it would help him at that age. In hindsight, that rationale was bogus. He has it; he deserved to know.

Next, I considered the following question: can a child—any child—understand what having Down syndrome means? Honestly, I found most adults, including educators and other professionals, knew next to nothing about Down syndrome.

My final consideration was how would I go about telling him. At the time, I couldn't adequately explain how Curious George was entrusted to navigate ships into New York harbor or fix the Hubble Telescope. How could I explain Down syndrome?

The day before the interviewer came to our house, I woke up at 2:48 A.M., convinced I was going to have an anxiety attack. What if some kid's parent from school saw me on television? What if he talked to his child about Thorin having Down syndrome? Then, what if the next day at school, that kid asked Thorin about having Down syndrome? Reason should have told me everyone already knew and, more importantly, maybe that had happened, but Thorin couldn't tell me.

My heart was racing during the next couple hours as I lay in bed, trying to turn this dilemma in my mind. Finally, unable to contain myself, I decided to wake up Ward.

"We have to tell him today!" I yelled, sitting upright in bed.

"What's happening?" came Ward's voice from under the covers.

"Wake up, wake up! We have to tell him he has Down syndrome!" I said.

At that point, I knew Ward did not actually have any idea what I was talking about, but he had heard me in this "we must do something" state before.

"Okay, settle down," Ward said in a resigned, tired husband way. "What time is it?"

"I'm not sure," I lied.

"Oh, God. Give me thirty minutes. Make coffee."

After much whispered debate, we decided we would both take the day to figure out how to tell him. Thoughtful planning and teamwork would be our key to success.

After Ward left for work, I told Thorin on my own. I wanted to be Team Us but I could not manage my anxiety. I believed the only way to not have an anxiety attack was by telling him that morning. I'm convinced if Little Ricky had Down syndrome, Lucille Ball would have done the same thing after Big Ricky went to the club.

As I watched Thorin from the doorway of the den, I thought, *This is the last minute he doesn't know he has Down syndrome.* He was watching *The Magic School Bus* and eating waffles. I walked in the room, swinging my arms in a way I had never done before.

"Hey, guy, dude, little man, buddy . . ." My voice trailed off, and I followed with maniacal smiling. "I'm going to turn the TV off for a bit so we can talk."

Like all males when notified they need to talk, he put his head in his hands and yelled, "No, no, no, no. Noooo!"

As I sat on the couch and looked thoughtfully at him across the room, I realized I had no concrete idea of what I was going to say. I looked at the floor and saw his substantial collection of Avenger action figures. A couple days before, we had all gone to the movie *Thor, The Dark World.* In fact, Thorin had worn his Thor costume to the theater.

"Have you ever heard the words *Down syndrome*?" I asked.

"No," he said.

I was surprised by Thorin's response. "Okay, have you ever felt like you were different from other people?"

"No," he said in an almost indignant tone, which shocked me.

"Okay. Well, I want to tell you something. Yeah . . . you . . . have a super power. It's called Down syndrome."

Thorin looked at me wide-eyed and flexed his biceps.

Things weren't going so bad, so I continued, "Down syndrome is an extra chromosome in your body . . ."

He started feeling around his mid-section.

"You can't see or feel your chromosomes; they are so small." I realized the scientific route was too abstract. "See, Down syndrome gives you almond-shaped eyes and a terrifically adorable flat nose. And, it gives you super powers. Some of your super powers are big love, photography, and . . . um . . . um . . . farting. It also made you a little small. Talking and being understood is hard for you right now, and learning some things takes more work."

Thorin nodded his head and smiled, signaling that he accepted all this information.

I leaned forward. "Not everyone sees your super power, so some people just see someone who needs help for some reason."

Thorin started laughing.

"The thing is . . . Daddy and I always wish we were better parents, but we never wish you didn't have your Down syndrome super powers."

"*Magic School Bus*?" he asked, directing me with his waffle-crusted fork to turn the television back on.

"Of course!" I said, relieved. And I was. My anxiety was gone.

I emailed Ward to tell him what I had done. I included that Thorin was fine, and now Down syndrome would be a lifelong conversation. When Ward wrote back, he told me it was okay; I did good.

I published that conversation with Thorin on *Huffington Post*. I received emails from around the world thanking me; however, I also got some crap. People who objected did so on the grounds that disability is not a super power. I do see the validity in that argument, but if Thorin didn't worship the Avengers, I wouldn't have used that explanation. It worked for Thorin, and I never suggested this was the answer for anyone else.

The things I chose to denote his super power were things most people can do—love, take pictures, and fart—which told him he was like everybody else. I didn't want Thorin to think Down syndrome is only what he cannot do. Later, I provided Thorin with a basic genetic explanation of Down syndrome. He told me to stop talking during my informational session.

———

At our next IEP meeting, we were accompanied by our advocate, Trisha. Aside from the usual crowd, a communication specialist and the behavioral specialist were also present. To the behavior specialist's credit, she did talk about Thorin's behavior as a response to not being understood and the class's behavior as infantilizing. Still, the divide between "him" and "them" was hard to reconcile. She was there to reinforce appropriate behavior, not change the mind-set of the class about people with Down syndrome. It would be like addressing sexual harassment in the workplace without acknowledging such a thing exists and hurts people.

Craig Joyce, the communication specialist who had named his company after himself and was always referred to formally, came across as confident, experienced, and knowledgeable. He made a pitch for an application that would change the way Thorin could participate in the classroom. I had spoken with him the day before, and he had made a compelling case to request incorporating that particular device into the IEP. "If we do that, it will make it easier for me the next time—here or at another school—to get other students the help they need." His presentation was so persuasive everyone in the room enthusiastically agreed to write that specific device into the IEP.

Next, we addressed a concern with Mrs. Dean, his special education case manager. Ward took the lead.

"We noticed on the communication log that Thorin leaves the classroom with you for forty-five minutes at a time, but it doesn't indicate what you do."

"Sometimes we walk around the school looking at things," she replied.

"You look at things? What kind of things?" I asked. I could feel Ward tapping my shoe as I talked.

"I set up things for him to take photos of."

"What?" asked Ward, alarmed.

"I took the flowers from the front office and put them in my room. I arranged them for him. He didn't want to do it, but then he did."

I wanted to say, "What a pedestrian composition, you fucking philistine!"

Ward was equally agitated. "We don't tell Thorin what to take photos of. That's his thing. Just his."

"Oh, it was fun!" she exclaimed, completely oblivious.

Joan Croft was thankfully not able to attend the meeting, but a new face, Ms. Shay, was there from the district. She jumped in.

"Mrs. Dean, what I'm hearing is Thorin's parents don't want you do that again."

Mrs. Dean made a pouty face but agreed. Next, she said Thorin didn't know the alphabet.

"Okay, that's not true," I said keeping my voice neutral.

The principal jumped in, "Mrs. Dean, tell us why you think that."

She pulled out a sheet of paper with the letters of the alphabet in no particular order on it.

"I said, 'Thorin show me the W,' and he couldn't. He couldn't show me any of the letters I asked for. He circled the wrong letters every time." She was completely satisfied with her documented findings.

"Can I see that a minute?" Ward studied the paper quickly then said, "Okay, I see what happened. He circled T-H-O-R-I-N. He circled the letters in his name."

The principal asked Ward for the sheet, "Mrs. Dean, he's right. It's his name."

"Oh, I didn't notice that," Mrs. Dean said. "Still, they weren't the right . . ."

Ms. Shay audibly sighed, "Okay, let's move on."

The school psychologist had joined the meeting late, missing the report from the behavior specialist.

"I have been checking in with Mrs. Mallory, the morning Ed Tech. Thorin continues to eat at the bad boy table."

"The what table?" I asked.

Laughing, the school psychologist said, "It's something I call it. It's a table for boys who act up."

Ward asked, "How long has he been there?"

"Weeks. There, it's easier to control the situation."

"What was he doing that he ended up there?" I asked.

Mrs. Mallory answered, "He takes kids' food packages or touches their food trays . . ."

The principal interrupted, "First, I don't ever want to hear the expression 'bad boy table' again. Second, Thorin can sit where he wants."

The fact the school psychologist thought it was amusing to segregate a group of boys was beyond me. I could see Thorin taking a food package to see what it was. It would have been hard for him to say, "Can I see that?" and be understood. I could also see him touching someone's tray to get a rise out of Mrs. Mallory. After all, that was expected behavior from Thorin; they were reinforcing negative attention.

The IEP meeting was a meeting of revelations. There were people in that room who had direct and profound impact on Thorin's well-being and didn't know what they were doing. And, we weren't the only ones who were noticing that.

—

Ward and I finally met with Superintendent Samuel. The meeting had been in the works after we had filed our formal complaint with the district regarding Sarge, the Ed Tech, but it had taken another couple of months to make it happen. Dr. Samuel wore a suit, conveying he was the guy who called the shots. Ward wore a sports jacket and tie, conveying calm and reason. I wore jeans and a T-shirt I had slept in, conveying discontent and depression. I had reached the end of my rope on patience. Thorin had been done wrong, and I was out for blood.

"I want an apology for what has happened to Thorin," I demanded.

Dr. Samuel looked at Ward then me, "That's not going to happen. No one is going to apologize. We don't do that."

"Why are you allowing women who were educated in the 1970s determine the fate of children with disabilities today?" I asked.

I saw Ward nod. We both waited.

"I'm going to tell you something, and if you tell anyone else, I'll say you're a liar. I can't do anything until these women retire. They have to leave and make room for others who know differently," the superintendent said.

I saw my hands were clutched. I felt a tight band in my chest and my head.

Ward said, "No rubber room, uh?"

Samuel chuckled, "You're not from Maine."

"Jersey."

"I can't move them. They're here."

I had no idea what they were talking about. The conversation was a back and forth between them. I noticed I was slouched in my chair with my legs spread in front of me. My head was against the chair back. I thought I might fall asleep.

When Ward and I were back in the car I asked, "What's a rubber room?"

"It's the room teachers report to when they're accused of misconduct. They get paid to do nothing. They're kept there instead of the classroom."

"What are you thinking?" I asked.

"I'm worried about you, Kari"

"Me, too."

***

Winter break was a welcome relief from school. Thorin spent his time going to movies and sledding with Ella and Evvy. Bubba had been in the hospital and was staying with us until she was ready to go home. Thorin liked crawling into bed to cuddle and read with her. It was good medicine for them both. It was hard not to notice how calm life was away from school.

When school restarted, the implementation of the communication device for Thorin to use in the classroom was finally beginning. I attended a training session with Thorin, Mrs. Holt, and his Ed Techs. The communication program was labor intensive. You had to push three buttons to get to a single word utterance. Thorin would not be able to use it functionally until he and his Ed Techs knew how to operate it. I shared my concerns with the Craig Joyce outside the training.

"Thorin needs something now."

"But this helps him with sentence structure. He needs that."

"First, he needs people to understand him. Right now he needs that."

A couple weeks later, I asked Thorin if he was excited about using the communication program.

He teared up, "No."

"No?"

"No."

"How about giving it more time?"

He didn't say anything. That night, Thorin got out his signing DVDs and started watching them. The next morning at breakfast, he signed rather than spoke.

I contacted Craig Joyce to tell him Thorin started signing at home. He seemed unwilling to entertain the fact Thorin was not happy. He emailed me back.

He may not be as excited as we are about the long-term prospect of being able to communicate effectively given what he is attempting. I would avoid asking questions that imply an option, especially if the "no" option is really not an option. I think that the device can be a very valuable language learning and communication tool. I think, and I hope that you do as well, it is important for him to learn to use it. We wouldn't ask "Do you want to brush your teeth? Will you wear your jacket today?" If we suggest it is an option, then he may choose not to.

The upshot for me reading the email was Thorin's thoughts and feelings were not important. I thought equating brushing teeth with learning a communication program that was as hard as articulating speech was a simplistic comparison to get what he wanted. The "why" of his defensiveness was difficult to understand.

Both Ed Techs and Mrs. Holt shared with me privately they thought the program was too much work. They found it frustrating. All of them agreed Thorin needed more immediate help, but no one wanted to tell a decision maker that. Mrs. Holt also shared she could not do enough for Thorin.

"I have so many children that I can't work individually with anyone. Thorin is in a speech group, but that's not enough."

"How do we do that?" I asked.

"A lot of parents get an outside speech therapist; that way, someone can work with only him. He needs that."

A week later, he was going to a second speech therapist after school, twice a week. Thorin was motivated and excited to go.

The demands of being an advocate at the school, helping my mom, and working were taking its toll. At the time, I felt like I was riding an endless wave. Sometimes, I was on top of it; other times, I was hit by it and held under. When my phone rang and I saw it was from the school—which was happening a couple times a week—I teared up, and my heart started racing. The usual compliant was Thorin wanted to come home because he was sick.

In January, Thorin said to me, "Help me more. Come school."

"Okay. Thorin, do you know what the problem is?"

"Yesith."

"Tell me, Sweetheart."

"It's me."

"Thorin, you are not the problem . . ."

"Yesith! Am!"

I was trying to hold it together, "It's them, Thorin." I said it. It was true.

We hugged each other for a long time.

"Thorin, I will come to school. I'll volunteer."

"Good! Now?"

"As soon as possible. I promise."

Mrs. Bruce said I could help at reading time. In the classroom, I was instructed to sit in a little area with a rug and a bookcase. The children rotated from different stations in the classroom. The first group was interested in my demographics.

One boy sat next to me and asked, "You're Thorin's mom?"

"I am."

"How old are you?"

"I'm old enough."

They all laughed. It was fun listening to them read. Thorin never made it over to my station before I left.

In the hall as I was leaving, an older boy who I did not know said, "Thorin hit me."

"I don't believe you!" I said, not breaking stride.

A stranger, a boy from an upper grade, saying that threw me. How far had Thorin's reputation migrated from his classroom? Had the boy noticed Thorin at the bad boy table? If Thorin had hit him, had the boy teased Thorin? Or, done something to warrant Thorin retaliating? How did the boy know who I was? As I sat in my car, I thought about my days in social work and the term *identified patient,* or IP. The IP was the person in the family who was the scapegoat for the dysfunction of the family. The term could be applied to any system where there is dysfunction, confusion, and denial. Thorin was the IP at school. If they could just get him to be different, everything would be better.

I started becoming anxious about one thing in particular: getting disruptive behavior disorder removed from Thorin's medical record, which had been diagnosed by Dr. Rachel the previous year. I found other people's obsession with his behavior pathological. And, it wasn't just about Thorin. According to the National Down Syndrome Society website, "at least half of all children and adults with Down syndrome face a major mental health concern during their life span."

Five out of the ten common mental health concerns listed for people with Down syndrome were behavioral. What if part of the issue was with the evaluation of people with Down syndrome in general? If we, as a culture, mistreat individuals by not including them and demeaning them, then they might not behave to our liking. What if people with Down syndrome were society's identified patient? If only they would stop being so upset at how they were treated.

I thought of Ethan Saylor, the man with Down syndrome who had been killed for refusing to leave the movie theater. Some reports cited he had a history of getting "upset" when he was touched. The reporting didn't specify what upset meant. I was also troubled that touching was equated with being manhandled by three aggressive security guards, and the fact it was considered noteworthy in the news coverage seemed to imply Ethan's Down syndrome had contributed to his death. I had seen how Thorin's behavior had contributed to him being identified as difficult rather than a victim of his circumstances.

Ward agreed with me about Thorin's diagnosis being a roadblock, so we made it a priority. After two meetings with Dr. Rachel and her consulting with the staff director at the clinic, Dr. Rachel was able to remove the diagnosis. She was understanding and compassionate and agreed his problem was the communication barrier rather than a behavioral problem. Thorin was not aggressive. She also helped us understand her point of view: "We work in the confines of a medical model. We aren't rewriting the historical treatment of people with Down syndrome, which has been abysmal. The problem lies with the person. That's the medical model."

On one of my volunteer days, I saw Thorin was ahead of me in the hall. I was going to catch up to him when I saw a boy come up to him and say something. Thorin stopped walking. He looked at the boy and shook his head no. The boy grabbed Thorin by the shoulder, causing Thorin to pull away and wave off the boy. Then, the boy slapped his thigh like he was calling for a dog and said, "Here, Thorin! Here, Thorin!"

I reached them quickly. Thorin ran. I turned to the boy.

"Don't ever do that again."

"What?"

"Don't even look at him," I said as I went to find Thorin.

Because Thorin and I didn't know the boy, nothing could be done. I made the case for better observation at an informal meeting with staff.

"You seem to know everything Thorin does, maybe you need to start looking at the other children more," I told his Ed Tech, Mrs. Shelby.

"He's the worst."

"Really? Thorin is the worst behaved child in class?"

"Yes."

Since volunteering, I saw several children misbehave. There was one boy who couldn't sit still and roamed the room, stopping to look at books or what other kids had on their desks. The teacher constantly had to ask him to sit down. The boy also talked loudly during class and interrupted the teacher and other children on a regular basis. The boys, in general, were very physical, whether it was chest bumping or hard slaps for high-fives. I saw one boy start to cry after a particularly rough hit. I witnessed one girl insist Thorin high-five her. He said no, and when that didn't work, he turned his back on her. She grabbed him by the arm, turning him back to her, and said, "You have to do it, Thorin!"

No one else seemed to see these things. Were they so intently focused on Thorin? I started wondering if the Hawthorne Effect was also at play. Thorin knew he was being watched. Was he modifying his behavior in response to being observed? I decided to talk to Mrs. Holt.

"Kids can be awful! Thorin is not the worst anything. This communication piece is holding up his progress. He needs to connect with the other kids," she said.

I nodded. She had a point. When I volunteered, the children often asked questions about Thorin: "What's his room look like?"; "Does he have books?"; "What's his favorite TV show?"; or "Does Thorin have a tie?"

Mrs. Holt continued, "I have a program I downloaded for Thorin and some other kids, Pictello. He can tell a story about himself in class. On the program, you can upload photos and write text with it. He loves photos!"

I talked to Mrs. Bruce who approved the presentation. We downloaded the program on Thorin's iPad at home and started working on the presentation. Ward, Thorin, and I had a blast putting together a story about Thorin. First, we made a list of what Thorin wanted the class to know: he likes helping Daddy cook; he likes the Avengers; he likes the beach; he has two dogs, Coco and Walt; he has a Bubba, an uncle, and an aunt; and he likes taking photos. Thorin took the photos for the presentation, and Ward and I helped him create sentences using his own words.

As we were wrapping up, Thorin said, "Wait! One more!"

He ran into his room.

I yelled, "Do you need help?"

"No! Stay!"

After a few minutes, he came into the kitchen dressed in his Thor costume, including helmet and hammer. He grabbed the iPad.

"Here! Here!" he said pointing to the camera. He pushed the icon for video.

"Do you want me to video tape you?"

"Yesith!" He took his place in front of me.

"Okay, action!"

He smiled and said, "I am Thor."

I stopped recording. "That's what you want them to know?"

He nodded his head and then danced around the kitchen.

"Well, Thorin, I think that's brilliant," Ward commented.

When Thorin and I went to the front of the class on the day of the presentation, he stopped me.

"Can't do it."

"Will you sit with me up here? I can do it," I told him.

"Okay."

I looked out at the classroom and said, "Has anyone ever been afraid of talking in front of a group?"

Everyone's hand went up, including Mrs. Bruce, who said, "I still get nervous teaching, Thorin. It's scary."

Thorin looked up at the class and said in a quiet voice as he pointed to the screen, "I did this."

The presentation went off without a hitch. There was wild clapping at the end, then Mrs. Bruce asked for questions. The first one was from one of the boys.

"Why can't we do fun stuff like that? I want to tell my story, too!"

"Thorin, why can't you talk?" asked another student.

Thorin hooked his thumb at me.

"First, Thorin can talk, but sometimes it's hard to understand him. He works really hard to be understood."

Another boy stood up and said, "I know why. My dad told me."

Thorin and I looked at each other. We both reflexively made a grimace.

"Is this okay, Thorin?" I asked.

Thorin smiled. "Yesith, okay."

The boy continued, "You have an extra cell in your body."

Thorin nodded his head; no more questions were asked. Thorin was thrilled at the response he received. He did the presentation later that week for family and friends.

Thorin's high was short-lived. He was up every night after the presentation. One night in particular, he couldn't go back to sleep. We sat in the den, watching Don Knotts in *The Incredible Mr. Limpet*, eating popcorn, and drinking juice. I called my mom the next morning and explained what was happening. She offered a sage observation: "He got a little taste of communicating. It's probably even harder now."

———

I surveyed everyone at school who had direct contact with Thorin about the communication device. It was not being used for its intended purpose—communicating with others—because it was too difficult to use and took too long to create a response. Instead, Thorin was inputting words from books in it. That sounded like busy work.

Ward and I sent an email to Ms. Shay, the principal, his teacher, Mrs. Holt, and the Ed Techs.

We are respectfully asking that use of the communication device be suspended immediately. Thorin expressed, again, after school yesterday that he is sad and mad. If we can reduce stress for Thorin, that is most important. Ward and I told Thorin he can take a break from using it, so let's have that start today. If that is an issue, please notify us ASAP.

Thank you,
Kari and Ward

The school staff listened to us. That night Thorin slept through until morning.

<hr>

Thorin's outside speech therapist had to change one of his appointment times to 2:30 P.M., which was twenty minutes before school ended. I made arrangements with his teacher and had notified the front office that I was picking up Thorin early that day. When I pulled in the parking lot, I saw the vice principal standing where the school buses parked, holding what looked like a cell phone from the 1990s, which I think must have been a walkie-talkie. As I walked toward the building, I saw a few Ed Techs coming from the sidewalk that ran along the street. I went into the office. The principal stood next to the both receptionists; no one said anything to me. Then, the office door flew open. Two more Ed Techs and the lunch lady filed in.

"Anything?" One of them said, then stopped short on seeing me. They all backed into each other with the last one squished against the closed door. One of the receptionists looked at me.

"What do you want?" she said in an aggravated tone.

"Um, I told you I was coming early for Thorin."

"Can you go get him?"

"Sure."

"Okay, bye!"

"Don't I have to sign in and get a pass?" The week before, I was reprimanded for not signing in and taking a pass.

"I'll sign you in!" offered the receptionist.

Then, the principal grabbed a pass and threw it at me. As I walked to find Thorin, I had the distinct feeling I had interrupted a posse. I got Thorin, and we went back to the office to return the pass and sign out.

Only the receptionists remained in the office. Thorin sat down and picked up a book while I signed out and handed in my pass. As I turned toward Thorin, I saw David, the other boy with Down syndrome, walk into the school. Mrs. Mallory, Thorin's former case manager, came around the corner as he walked into the hall. She immediately yelled in an angry tone at him, "I bet you thought that was funny!"

Thorin turned in his seat, his mouth making a little O. She kept yelling at David. I turned to look at the receptionists who had their heads turned conveniently down toward the desk. I felt awful for David. Mrs. Mallory's tirade seemed endless. I wanted to go to him. I didn't; I wimped out. I took Thorin by the hand, and we left. As we were walking to our car, I saw a parent from the school. She was out of breath and holding her side. She looked like she was about to cry.

"Hey, are you okay?" I asked her.

"Oh! Have you seen a boy . . ."

It wasn't a posse I saw; I had seen a rescue party.

"He's inside! We saw him!" I told her.

Someone—I couldn't see who—yelled at the parent from the front door, "He's in here!" Then the woman went running toward the school.

I experienced firsthand a situation I found to be disturbing. A situation I could imagine happening to Thorin. And, I didn't do anything; I was awful. I deferred to who was in charge. I did what I thought was the next best thing. I private messaged David's mother: "I'm checking in about what happened at the school. Thorin and I were in the front office when David came back to the school. I wanted to run and hug him. If you want to call me, please do. Very scary."

She wrote back: "Thanks for your message. I appreciate it a lot. Yes, very scary. From what I understand, though, he never got out of the Ed Tech's sight."

Her reply completely threw me. I wrote back: "I don't think that version is true. Can we talk?"

When we talked on the phone, I told her what I had witnessed. She said she would contact the school for more information and let me know.

A couple days later, I discovered the parent who was so distraught as we were leaving that day was also a substitute Ed Tech. She had been David's Ed Tech that day. He clearly had not been in her eyesight the entire time. I never heard from David's mother; in fact, she and I never spoke after that.

I tried to imagine some alternate scenario for what I saw, but nothing else made sense. Two other parents were intimately involved in what had happened, the Ed Tech and David's mom. Was I really the only one troubled about the school lying?

I told Ward, "I don't know what we should do."

"Kari, we can't do anything. No one has a problem with it but you . . . and me, of course."

"But the principal and the others know I was there. They have to know I saw it."

"Exactly. If you end up dead, I will assume it was by their hand and direct the police."

There was a bright hope in one person at the school. Ms. Alice was actually teaching Thorin. She conveyed not only to Ward and me but also to Thorin that he could learn. She learned how to sign all the key words for phonics instruction, so Thorin could sign the word and say the word. She knew signing gave Thorin confidence and talking was a fearful proposition. The multisensory instruction made a huge difference in Thorin's reading. Thorin had stopped reading at home. I think the discrepancy between what little they expected of him at school and the more accurate assessment of him at home was too much. After Ms. Alice's learning intervention, Thorin began pulling out books at home.

I received a lovely email from Ms. Alice recently. She was shocked I would credit her with so much of Thorin's success. She shared that he made her a better teacher and other students continue to benefit when the phonics instruction is delivered using the multimodal approach she learned with him.

Now that Thorin's reading seemed to be moving forward, his communication needs had to be addressed. Mrs. Holt, the speech therapist, agreed to meet with me when I talked to Craig Joyce about using a more effective and accessible device. The district finally agreed the device was not suitable but couldn't give Thorin a new device because it was in the IEP. In preparation for the meeting, I had done research on the program. A major criticism is that the learning curve is three to four years. This application, as suspected, was never appropriate for Thorin's immediate communication needs.

Mrs. Holt shared with me moments before the meeting in a regretful tone, "I have no backbone."

I realized I had to boost her confidence. "No worries! I'll present the criticisms. You just back me up, okay?"

"Okay!"

The meeting with Craig Joyce quickly devolved into him yelling at me. He was offended I would suggest he had made a mistake. He was a real prima donna.

"I am telling you we want to change course to a device that's easier for Thorin to use."

He went from just yelling at me to spitting unintentionally on me, due to the fact he was foaming at the mouth. I looked at Mrs. Holt to see if she was okay. If normal talking freaked her out, she must be a complete mess thanks to the yelling. She didn't utter a word during the meeting.

As he was still yammering away, I stood up and said, "We're done here. I'll figure it out another way." We weren't getting anywhere, and his spittle was nauseating.

After he left, Mrs. Holt said, "I'm sorry! He intimidates me. I couldn't talk."

"It's okay. It wouldn't have made a difference anyway."

The next week, the district found another communication specialist to say Craig Joyce was wrong. The new communication specialist recommended an application that was easier to use. She would show Thorin the application to see if he liked it before implementing it. That same day, I spoke with Thorin's teacher, Mrs. Bruce, who was less than helpful. I asked how he was doing educationally.

"I don't know. I'm not really his teacher."

"You're not?"

"No."

"Well, he thinks you are."

"Oh, that's so nice!" I wanted to punch her. She felt no sense of duty to Thorin who was a student in her classroom.

Mrs. Dean was also increasingly becoming a bigger obstacle to Thorin's education. She had been doing assessments with Thorin but admitted she didn't understand him when he talked. Still, she wanted to present her findings at the year-end IEP meeting.

Thorin shared with me at breakfast one morning, "No more Mrs. Dean."

"Oh, boy."

"Please."

Ms. Shay, from the district office, seemed sympathetic to our concerns about Thorin's education. I asked if she would attend a staff meeting. She was happy to attend and also said she would push Mrs. Dean to give concrete reporting on what she was doing with Thorin.

Before the meeting, Mrs. Dean offered to meet with Thorin and me. Both Mrs. Holt and the occupational therapist sat in with us, so they could update me before the meeting as well.

Mrs. Dean said to Thorin, "Want to show off for your mom?"

"Okay."

"Alright, what have we learned? Let's do it together."

In unison she and Thorin said, "4, 3, 2, 1! Blast off!"

"Thorin, you forgot to jump out of your seat on blast off! Let's do it again!"

"No, please don't," I said. Seeing it once was disturbing enough.

"We have to! He didn't get out of his seat."

They did the routine one more time. Mrs. Holt and the occupational therapist looked sad.

"Mrs. Dean, Thorin counts to fifty at home."

"Um, not here."

I bet not here. Mrs. Dean had the bar set too low. Thorin went back to his classroom.

Ms. Shay was true to her word. She pressed Mrs. Dean for details on Thorin's progress. In official mode, Mrs. Dean referred to Thorin as a cognitive profile. The fourth time she did it, I interrupted.

"Mrs. Dean, he has a name." Then I turned to Ms. Shay and said, "Make her stop."

Ward put his hand on my back.

"Mrs. Dean, I want you talk about some of Thorin's specific gains, please," Ms. Shay requested.

"He can hold a book right-side up and he knows words go from left to right."

I knew Thorin was reading pre-literacy books at home, and Ms. Alice was working with him on reading as well.

"He knew those things before he got to kindergarten," Ward said.

Ward and I refuted the remainder of her reporting as well below his capacity. Ms. Shay suggested adjourning with the suggestion that a formal end-of-the-year IEP be held with the expectation that Thorin's skill levels would be increased. Also given school was ending soon, a proper and supportive summer session needed to be determined. Everyone left the room except for Mrs. Holt, the occupational therapist, and me. I put my head on the table and started sobbing. They sat quietly with me. When I lifted my head, I saw both of them had tears in their eyes.

"Does she hate him?" I asked referring to Mrs. Dean

They told me there had been so many complaints about her regarding the children she worked with that the district had moved her caseload to other case managers. Mrs. Dean had fought to keep Thorin, and they had agreed.

I emailed Ms. Shay requesting Thorin have a new case manager. She wrote back quickly agreeing to the change.

Thorin's new case manager was Jay Trask. He was retiring in a month after a thirty-year career and had been moved from a high school to Thorin's school that week—that couldn't be a good sign. It made me wonder what Mr. Trask had done at the high school since they were transferring him to an elementary school to be a case manager for students who had disabilities. I had also heard Mrs. Mallory, Thorin and David's former case manager, was also retiring. Maybe there wasn't a rubber room in the school district, but Superintendent Samuel's words came back to me: "I can't do anything until they retire."

I also hoped the district moved Mr. Trask to say they had a warm body handling case services for children with disabilities at the school rather than he was menace to children. That's how all the districts tactics had affected my expectations for Thorin: "Gee, I hope he's just a do-nothing and not a dangerous pervert."

When I went to see Mr. Trask, he told me in a confused and sad sort of way, "I have no idea what I'm doing."

"Oh! That has to be hard."

"It is. The kids I met are nice, and they hang out in my office. Thorin could do that, too."

"Well, let me think about that. Do you want me to take the lead on ideas regarding Thorin?"

"Yes! Thank you!"

"No prob."

I went to see the principal and reported, "Mr. Trask says he doesn't know what he's doing."

"He does know."

"But he said he doesn't."

"He's wrong."

———

I ordered a book prior to the end-of-the-year IEP meeting titled *The Paraprofessional's Handbook for Effective Support in Inclusive Classrooms*. The book is written by a paraprofessional, which is another term for an Ed Tech, and is considered a resource for best practices. I learned implementation of inclusion is often facilitated by the paraprofessional or Ed Tech, and that person modifies the curriculum given to them by the teacher.

I wanted Ward and me to be better prepared to discuss what we wanted for Thorin. The school said they were inclusive, but the reality was that they had no guiding philosophy, no living document. They had no clue other than sticking a child with a disability into a regular classroom and calling it good. We had learned too late that for inclusion advocates like Trisha, Thorin was cannon fodder to lob at the school. She was trying to force change through IEPs—too bad if Thorin was the collateral damage. Ward and I had relieved her of her duty. We wanted a working document; a plan that said *this* is inclusion.

The meeting went better than expected. Ms. Shay ran the show and called people to account. Mrs. Bruce could not get away with saying Thorin was not her student. But what she did do was lie about her role; she said she had been facilitating inclusive practices. When asked if she had provided class plans to Ms. Alice for modification, she said she did provide them.

Ms. Alice responded, "That's not true. You do not give me lesson plans."

Go Ms. Alice! From the look on her face, I could see she was as about done with Mrs. Bruce as we were.

Ms. Shay asked, "Why aren't you providing the plans?"

Mrs. Bruce didn't say anything, but Ms. Alice did. "You don't do your plans until the day of class."

Ms. Alice went on to explain she had facilitated inclusive classrooms in the past. She outlined how an inclusive classroom operated and explained the roles of the teachers and Ed Techs. She was clearly excited by being in a role she was supremely qualified to fill. Her enthusiasm was contagious. I would ask questions of her from the paraprofessional book that I had on my lap. Ms. Shay, the district person, took copious notes, smiled, nodded, and said, "Great stuff!" I saw the principal, who was seated to my left, lean in to write down the title of the book I was holding.

As the meeting drew to a close, I became less enthusiastic. The responsibility of planning the classroom and coordinating with the summer school teachers was given to Mrs. Bruce and Mr. Trask— Mrs. Do Nothing and Mr. Know Nothing. Ward and I tried to be positive. Ms. Alice had been assigned as Thorin's Ed Tech for summer school, which would begin in a month and half.

———

Two days later, I was called into a meeting at work and told I had been laid off along with sixteen other people.

———

Given how plans in the past hadn't shaken out the way promised, I went to the school the day before summer school started while

Thorin visited with Bubba. I found the summer teacher, and she told me she hadn't heard from Mrs. Bruce or Mr. Trask about a plan. I knew those two wouldn't be able to pull that kind of coordinating off. Ms. Alice should have been placed in charge, but she hadn't; even though she had more education and experience, she had the title Ed Tech.

In lieu of receiving plans for Thorin, this summer school teacher had taken it upon herself to create a plan for Thorin. Each day, Thorin would be allowed to attend the morning meeting, and in the late morning, he would join the regular class for an experiential science project. The remaining three hours of the day, he would work alone with an Ed Tech in another room.

When I heard the plan, I notified Ms. Shay and the principal that Thorin would not be attending summer school. We fell for it again! I think one of our worst characteristics as parents was our enduring hope the school would do right by Thorin. We were banging our heads against a brick wall. The school could not do better by Thorin whether it was because of their ignorance or their resistance. Or both.

When Ms. Alice arrived for summer school, she heard what happened. Then, she did an amazing thing. In forty-five minutes, she created an inclusive summer experience that she got the teachers to happily accept. The next day, Thorin and I went to check it out. He agreed to try it.

Soon the insomnia, the crying, the school refusal, and wetting himself started. He began wetting the bed at home, too. I was called to the school by one of the receptionists who told me Thorin had wet himself three times that morning.

Ms. Alice was out sick that day, and I was met by a substitute aide. She explained what had transpired during the morning. As Thorin went to get his things from his locker, she said kindly, "I don't think he wants to be here." The simplicity of her statement struck me. That may have been the truest thing ever expressed about Thorin in the school.

When he got into the car with me, Thorin said, "I will wet and wet to leave."

"Oh, Thorin . . ."

He cried, "No, Mommy! You do more for me, please."

That was a mouthful for any kid but more so for Thorin. It was if the sheer frustration of two years were pushed out of his mouth, demanding I do something.

I told Thorin I had to make a quick call. I stepped out of the car and moved several feet away. Ward answered.

"I want to tell Thorin right now that we are homeschooling."

"Do it."

"We're okay?"

"We're okay."

When I got back in the car, I turned to face Thorin. "Okay you don't have to go to school anymore."

"Good! Thank you!"

"We'll do school at home. You can learn reading, writing, and math, everything with me."

It was done. It felt wonderful. That calm that had eluded me for so long was back. That night, Ward and I talked about the logistics of homeschooling. We had started saving money ever since Thorin came into our life. That money was being put aside for his future when we weren't here.

Ward pointed out, "You don't have a job. Thorin's future is now."

"Can we do this?"

"Yes. You homeschool. We live on less money. That's not such a big problem."

We rented and didn't have car payments. All of sudden, it seemed like a low-risk proposition with high rewards.

I emailed the school the next morning that Thorin was not returning and would be homeschooled. I went to the school alone to get Thorin's materials from Mrs. Holt and Ms. Alice. Mrs. Holt handed me his speech folder.

"Tell Thorin I will miss him, okay?"

"Of course I will."

Ms. Alice handed me his writing and reading folders. She also gave me a plastic bag filled with laminated cards, each with a different word on them.

"He knows these words. You can build on this. I really wanted it to work."

"I know. You did a great job!" I reassured Ms. Alice.

That evening, my mom came over to our house. She and I stayed up late, talking.

"Everything happened to bring you to this moment. Don't worry about anything," she told me.

"Really?"

"Yes, that's how God works. He brings you to a place you're supposed to be."

Top: Thorin busy at work; Bottom: Photo by Thorin

CHAPTER EIGHT

Funny How Life Happens

When I explained to Thorin we were homeschooling, he had two questions.

"I call you Kari?"

I laughed. I wasn't expecting that question.

"If that's important to you, sure," I said.

"Thanks you, Mom."

"Who the teacher?" he asked.

I wasn't expecting that question either. I didn't see myself as the teacher but more like a coworker. I had no frame of reference for this new model of our relationship.

"No one is the teacher?" I said.

"No! Who the teacher?"

"We could both be the teacher?"

"No!"

"We are both the student," I offered.

"No! Who the teacher!" he screamed it.

I realized public education is a potent force, particularly when removed.

"You need to learn reading, writing, and math. I have to figure out how to help you by learning how to help you. So we're both learning."

Thorin didn't have a response.

"Thorin, I am not sure what I am doing, yet."

"No!"

"I am learning, too. I don't want to be a teacher. I want us to be a team."

Again, Thorin didn't respond.

"Can we be a team? Can we try?"

"Okay, Kari."

Luckily, Maine had several resources for homeschooling: Christian-based and secular organizations, religious and secular homeschooling cooperatives, Facebook groups offering classes, fieldtrips, and group playdates. I learned there were homeschoolers and unschoolers—and those in between. I felt excited and overwhelmed.

We briefly checked out one of the homeschool cooperatives where families join together for classes and social time. Everyone was pleasant and laid back. I needed pleasant and structured. This was a huge leap for us. I wanted a safety net.

I discovered a nonprofit Christian ministry, HOME, dedicated to supporting homeschools in Maine. They didn't care if we were religious. They also had an informational workshop for new homeschoolers the next week.

It took place at a church an hour away. When we arrived, we found a seat in a pew in the back. The presentation was already going, so I started taking notes. After the speaker finished, he asked for questions. He answered some, and his wife, who was seated at the reception table in the back of the church, answered others.

I whispered to Ward, "Why isn't she up there, too?"

"He's the head of the household."

"Really?" I wasn't entirely convinced that was the accurate explanation, but Ward was having fun with the idea. They didn't care if we were religious, but, apparently, that didn't stop us from stereotyping them.

He poked me in the ribs. "Now you're going to have to start listening to me," he whispered.

I snorted, "I don't think so."

"Shhh, woman!"

After the meeting, Ward and I introduced ourselves to Ed and Kathy, the couple who ran HOME. "I emailed you about visiting for a curriculum consult," I said.

"We'd love to have you. Just let us know when," said Kathy.

A week later, we visited their bookstore. Kathy asked Thorin questions about what he liked. She asked me how he learned best.

"I would say Thorin's a visual and kinesthetic learner."

She turned to Thorin. "You like to learn by doing, Thorin?"

"I do."

Kathy's energy was calm and confident. She suggested Thorin go outside with her grandchildren and Ed. Ward asked if he could go, too.

"Kathy, I don't know what I'm going to do," I confessed.

"That's okay. This is time for you to learn, too. You're going to figure it out, and what's best is that you get to do it with your child."

"You always knew this is what you were going to do."

"Always."

"I didn't. School was so painful for Thorin."

"I hear that a lot."

"I really need help."

"That's why we're here."

While everyone outside helped load up firewood, Kathy suggested some math and writing texts. She cautioned me to buy only a few things and told me that I didn't have to figure it all out now.

On the first day of homeschooling, I set up an area on the dining room table for Thorin and me to sit. I thought we could look at the curriculum then do a couple pages of math. I was chipper and prepared. I should have also noticed it looked a lot like school.

"Yay, homeschooling!" I said calling to Thorin.

He came in the room wearing underpants and his Thor cape.

"Go get clothes on, please," I said enthusiastically.

"No, tanks."

"Please, go get clothes on," I repeated with somewhat less enthusiasm.

"No," Thorin said as he sat down.

Why did I think he had to wear clothes that morning? I decided because he couldn't call the shots. Look at everything I was doing for him! Where was that coming from?

Without thinking I said, "You have to have clothes on!" I didn't sound like a coworker; I sounded like a dictator.

Thorin ended up staying in his room all day in his underpants and cape. I cried into a pillow in the bedroom. I couldn't understand what was happening.

I told Ward when he got home. He reassured me that it would get better.

The next morning, Thorin came out naked.

"Okay, go get clothes on, now!"

"No, no, no!"

Yuck, I didn't want him sitting on anything.

"Yes!"

"Funny! No!"

"I'll show you funny! Get in your room!"

"Good!" he said and went stomping off.

The next day was the same. Between the crying and yelling, which now both of us were doing, I was exhausted. I wondered if we had made a colossal mistake, so I called my mom. When I told her about Thorin's nudity, she revealed a surprising bit of family history.

"Your father was a closet nudist. He said it made him feel free. I made him carry a dish cloth around the house."

"What?"

"Your father liked nothing better than being buck naked."

"Okay, please stop."

"Maybe this isn't going to work," she said.

It was one thing for me to think that, but I didn't want to hear that from someone else, especially my mom.

Pleading I told her, "Please don't say that."

"It doesn't sound good, Kari," she said definitively.

I didn't want to say something I would regret. "Okay, I have to go."

It was 9:45 A.M., and I was still in my pajamas. He'd beaten me. I hoped I wouldn't be running around naked the next day. I decided we had to get out of the house. *Think, Kari! Where could we go?* It took another cup of coffee to jog my memory of something Kathy had said: "Thorin's interests should direct what you learn." It was as if I had been visited by the hologram of Obi-Wan Kenobi.

I walked into Thorin's room and found him dressed in pajamas.

"Did you know there's a monster museum in town?"

He looked at me suspiciously. "Yeah?"

"No, really. It's called the International Cryptozoology Museum, which basically means monsters."

"Yesith!"

"They have a rule: everyone wears clothes."

"Sure!"

When we walked into the museum, it was indeed filled with monsters. A replica of Big Foot was just inside the doorway. An attractive woman who looked to be in her thirties with black hair, made-up eyes, and tattoos came over to us.

"Hello! Welcome! I'm Jenny, and that's my husband, Loren. We run the museum!"

"Hi! We're homeschoolers!"

"We love homeschoolers!"

"Wow!" I exclaimed.

"Wow!" Jenny added.

Even Thorin joined the exclamation party. "Wow!"

Jenny was born to be an educator. She exuded enthusiasm in everything she shared with us about the exhibits. Among three packed rooms, we saw hair from an Abominable Snowman, Yeti scat, and a doll made to look like a Sasquatch baby. Thorin was entranced with the museum and Jenny.

"I'm so glad we came here!" I said.

"I'm glad, too! You're both so lucky getting to learn together all day. If we had a child, I would homeschool."

I forgot there were people who wanted to be home with their children all day. I had never been that person. As Thorin was looking at the Minnesota Ice Man, Jenny came up to me with a T-shirt from their gift store.

"Can I give this to Thorin?"

"Really? Are you sure?"

"Yes, I wanted to make sure it was okay first. I love how excited he is to learn."

"Of course! We were supposed to come here today!"

"I know!"

As we left, I got another idea. The front part of the building was the Green Hand Bookshop.

"Thorin you want to go into this bookstore? They have the coolest stuff. Maybe you could find a book you like."

"Sure!"

We found the children's section. Thorin was pulling out books right and left. He found one on Frankenstein and went off to sit in an overstuffed chair for further examination. I found a small book with the title *A Ghost Named Fred*. Thorin loved ghost stories. I was surprised to see it was by Nathaniel Benchley. It was an "I Can Read Book" from 1968. I hadn't flipped through any of the pages but I loved it.

"Thorin! Look at this one! *A Ghost Named Fred*! It's by Nathaniel Benchley! He wrote the *Off Islanders*! His son wrote *Jaws*!"

Waving me off, he said, "No."

"Bubba loves Nathaniel Benchley!"

"Let's see," he said skeptically.

We sat together on the chair going from page to page.

"Yes?"

"Yesith. This, too?" he said holding up the Frankenstein book.

"Yes!"

I couldn't wait to tell Ward and my mom about the day. I rode that high all the way until the next morning when Thorin came to the dining room, naked, and informed me, "No school!"

The next morning as I lay in bed thinking about my day, I felt tears. When I heard Thorin's voice from the other room, I started crying. I then counted how many hours before I could go back to bed. I called my mom.

"Can I bring him there?"

"For how long?"

"I'll come back before he turns ten."

I needed help. I emailed Kathy, the cofounder of HOME, when I got back to our place.

Thorin says no to everything. [I decide not to divulge the nudity.] *It is day five of refusing and arguing, and I hit a wall. I want this to work. I think he is exercising his independence. And I want to send him to military school today. That is sort of a joke. Ha, ha. I am hoping I am not the worst homeschooling mother ever. Help! Thank you, Kari*

Seventeen minutes later—I couldn't help staring at the clock—I received a response from Kathy.

Hi Kari, How old is Thorin? I would suggest that you give me a call, so that we can talk this through. It could be a number of things. I would be happy to help!

We scheduled a call for that afternoon.

"What do you think the problem is, Kari?"

Shades of The Pee Whisperer emerged.

"Me."

"I'm glad you see it that way."

I filled her in on the details, including how I had always worked outside the home before beginning to homeschool.

"Oh! You two are experiencing a huge life transition. I wouldn't focus on curriculum right now."

"What do I do with him all day?"

"Cuddling on the couch and reading is always fun."

Cuddle on the couch? I don't know how much of that I did before. And, he'd have to wear clothes for me to entertain that idea.

"Okay," I said as I wrote it down. "What else?"

"How about cooking?"

"Huh, well, I don't cook. Ward cooks."

"Oh, my. Thorin needs to learn how to cook. Don't you want him to be capable and independent?"

She was right! And, I don't think she was talking just about a kid with Down syndrome.

"I guess we could learn together?" I offered, feigning enthusiasm.

"There you go! That would be good for both of you," Kathy responded with actual enthusiasm.

"Okay, I can do that," my voice sounded more confident. "Anything else?" I almost sounded cheery.

"How about cleaning together? You do know all this is learning, right?"

"Okay! I like that!" I succeeded in actual enthusiasm.

"Focus on what Thorin likes. The monster museum was a good idea."

I thought to myself as Kathy kept talking, *Thank you, Obi-Wan!*

Kathy also suggested once we started using curriculum to not make it like school. She reminded me, "Thorin hated school. You don't have to sit at the table. Learning happens everywhere."

The next morning, I asked, "Do you want to bake a cake?"

"Yesith!"

"Okay, get dressed; we're going to the store!"

I bought cake pans, cake mix, and ready-made frosting. I didn't see any reason to make it from scratch. Mixing anything in a bowl was going to be a challenge for me. Thorin picked out blue frosting with sprinkles. We listened to Johnny Cash and made a two-layer cake. It was delicious.

Being a stay-at-home parent who homeschooled was never being off-duty. It was a full-time job with overtime! It took energy, ingenuity, and creativity to be with a child all day long. I regretted every judgmental thought I'd ever had about a stay-at-home parent. Kathy was right: This was a huge transition for both of us. I was learning as much as Thorin, and most of it was on the fly. Thorin was still out of sorts and cranky. He was processing a horrible year of school and testing the limits with me. This was all going to take time. It would not be a smooth transition; there would be bumps and starts and do-overs. In hindsight, it makes perfect sense we butted heads.

One particularly crabby morning, I took Thorin out to lunch at 10:30. I hoped being outside the house would limit our bickering. Thorin, on the other hand, must have seen the public venue as a more effective way to get under my skin. He munched away on his grilled cheese, stopping only to say in a really loud voice every so often, "Hi, Bad Mommy!"

What a jerk! I sat with my head down, perusing a local weekly newspaper. I was reading the listings, looking for anything to take him to. The moment he said "Hi! Bad Mommy!" for the seventh time, a tear dropped from my eye onto the words "Does your child like make-believe?" It was an ad for a theater class starting that afternoon at the Children's Museum and Theatre of Maine.

"Thorin we're taking the rest to go."

"No, not!"

"Would you like to go to a theater class?"

He stopped mid-bite. "Yeah!"

I called the museum, and there was still room for him in the class. I asked to speak to the teacher.

"Hello, this is Jamie!"

"I'm calling about the theater class starting today. Um . . . my son has Down syndrome," I sounded tentative.

"Okay," she answered, like she heard this all the time.

"Is that a problem?" *Good grief! I'd been brainwashed by years of schooling!*

She laughed, "No, of course not!"

"He has a hard time talking or being understood." It felt like I was trying to talk her out of taking him.

She responded quickly, "We have students whose first language isn't English."

"Okay, see you later!"

When we arrived at the museum, Jamie was at the front desk to greet kids for the class. Thorin stood with them, away from me. A few minutes later, I watched Thorin follow Jamie and the other children upstairs.

I said to the woman at the front desk, "Can I wait here?"

"You can but you don't have to."

What should I do? Thorin just went off with a stranger and no aide.

"I better stay."

The woman smiled at me. "Sure. That's fine."

An hour and half later, Thorin appeared. He was so excited; he seemed ready to levitate. "How was it?"

"Great, Mom!"

When I talked to Ward that night, he told me that I did a good job. He also gave Thorin and me aprons he had bought.

⸻

Thorin and I started having breakfast with Bubba a couple times a week. One morning at our favorite diner, I noticed Thorin's attention was drawn away from his pancakes to the table behind us. First, he was smiling then he wasn't. He was frowning. I looked and saw three guys, about eighteen years old, who were taking turns looking at Thorin and laughing. The boys weren't trying to engage a cute kid in the next booth; they were literally pointing and laughing at a boy with Down syndrome. They were talking low enough that I couldn't hear what caused the outbursts of laughter. Thorin put his head down. I put my arm around his shoulder.

"I've got this. Don't worry."

I stared at the two facing me until one of them pulled his eyes away from Thorin and saw me. My expression? Imagine Heath Ledger as the Joker. That's when it hit him: *Holy shit, that lady is going to kick my ass!* He blanched and looked down at his plate. I couldn't hear what he said to the others, but their behavior stopped abruptly. They didn't look at our table once after I gave them the evil eye.

I turned to Thorin and said, "They're jerks. Don't mind them, okay?"

He nodded and went back to eating. My mom asked what happened. I quietly told her.

"What assholes!" she said.

We finished eating and decided to go to the park a couple blocks away. My mom and I sat on one of the benches, talking while Thorin played. About ten minutes later, those same guys showed up at the park. When they saw us, they moved behind a large area of bushes to pass around a Hacky Sack rather than play out in the field directly behind us.

I'm a believer in signs, and this was an opportunity to explain why their behavior was wrong. It was also something I could have never done at Thorin's school—at least not without getting permission and talking it to death beforehand with three staff people. So, I walked over to them. The guy who I had engaged with my menacing stare saw me and immediately looked down at the ground.

"Hey, I noticed all of you staring at my son in the restaurant earlier."

One of them said with a sneer, "What are you talking about?"

"You were all staring at my son and . . ."

Before I finished, one of them walked toward me with his chest out, chin up, and arms stretched out.

"We don't know what you are talking about, okay?" he said as the other two laughed.

Seriously? How did I get here? I'm a middle-aged woman being threatened by jerks who made fun of my son. I walked away confused and disgusted.

When I got back to the bench my mom said, "You have to be careful. I was worried one of them was going to hurt you!"

"I don't want to be careful anymore."

———

At the next theater class, I dropped Thorin off and left the building like all the other parents did. As I was leaving, I asked the receptionist, who I now knew to be Molly, "You have my number, right?

"I do!"

"Are there any other exits?"

"Just that one," she said, pointing to the front door.

"What if Thorin got away?"

"We haven't lost anyone yet. Try not to worry."

She was right. I didn't have to worry there. Nothing bad had happened. Besides, Thorin liked being independent. He didn't need an Ed Tech to assist him, and there was a whole new world to explore. But, I needed to trust him.

On the way home, I asked Thorin what other classes he wanted to take.

"Ballet," he replied.

"Really? I didn't know that!"

"Love ballet."

I knew he was interested but not to the degree he would want to take a class. We had watched a documentary on ballet, which Thorin had watched more than once by himself. Also he loved *The Nutcracker*. I found Spotlight Dance and Performing Arts Center through a friend of mine whose daughters danced. I called Heather, the director, and explained to her Thorin had asked to take ballet and he had Down syndrome.

"Okay, I see a couple potential issues."

Here it comes, I thought. *What will be the problem?*

"Uh, huh," I cautiously replied.

"We don't have just ballet for his age group, so it would be ballet, jazz, and tap. Also, he's going to be the only boy in the class."

"Oh, I'm sure that's fine! Thank you!" The world outside of school was so much easier to navigate. No one seemed to care if Thorin had Down syndrome. He was welcome. He was included. He wasn't a problem.

At the final theater class, the children performed for their parents and anyone else they invited. Ward took time off from work so we could both be there. Bubba wanted to go, but between her walker and the amount of walking, it would have been too much for her. When we walked in, Thorin was in his costume and makeup, sitting in the audience. Jamie walked over.

"Thorin said he doesn't want to perform today."

Ward turned toward Thorin. "No, Buddy?"

"No, Dad."

I asked, "Are you sure, Honey?"

"Sure."

I'd learned my lesson when it came to pressuring and simply said, "Okay."

The three of us sat together during the performance. His teacher, Jamie, reminded everyone there was a new class starting the next month.

"Thorin do want to do that?" I asked.

"Yesith!"

I talked to Jamie on the way out. I told her Thorin wanted to be in the next class.

"Great! Sometimes it's about the journey," she offered.

———

During the months leading up to leaving public school, Thorin had become a different child. He had frequent insomnia. He had crying jags and angry outbursts. He suffered regression on all levels: wetting the bed; things he once did were difficult again; and not wanting to read at home. He stopped taking photographs. And, he stopped growing. Thorin had stayed the same height for nine months.

I needed to slow down things at home. I needed to understand how Thorin processed information. I noticed he took the path of least resistance. When working on his reading one day, I observed he said "that" for "hat" or "down" instead of "away."

I asked, "Are you guessing?"

"Yesith!" he responded cheerfully.

"Did you guess at school?"

"Yesith!"

I slapped my hand on the table, "From now on we live in No Guessing Zone. We'll sound out the words instead."

I remembered Kathy's advice about using Thorin's interests, so I created reading material suited just for him. I titled the sheets "Thorin's Super Awesome Sentences!" The sentences had meaning for Thorin: "Thor eats cake with Iron Man"; "Spider Man can make blue cake"; and "Hulk likes smash cake." There was also Thorin's Super Great Cake Sentences, which were hyperfocused on cake, no Avengers. "Let's make a cake! Come look at the cake. Did you make the cake? Who will eat the cake?" And, "I had too much cake."

I learned Thorin needed more time to respond. Like many parents, I was so quick to interrupt his silence because I didn't realize he needed more "think time" before answering. Once I made that discovery, I would count to myself while Thorin thought: ten seconds, twenty seconds, thirty seconds, and, once, even forty seconds. What I thought was dead space was actually processing time that allowed Thorin to answer correctly.

Another thing I slowly realized is that learning was a fearful proposition for Thorin. He had been made to feel dumb in the past. When we would start anything new, I would casually take his hand in mine. It worked! That touch, that reassurance, made a difference. Even if he didn't get it right, he was still willing to work until he did.

We began to learn antonyms. Thorin grasped those for "hot," "up," "out," and "down," but for more complex words, he seemed to get confused.

"Cloudy," I said.

"Movie star," he responded, which totally perplexed me.

I decided to keep giving him words, thinking something had to give. I finally figured out what was going on when he replied "Project Runway" after I said the word "young."

"Are you saying something you know I like instead of 'I don't know'?"

"I am."

"Did you do that at school?"

"I did!"

At that point, I began to understand his strategy at school: get them to stop asking anything.

I looked at Thorin smiling and told him, "It's okay not to know something. From now on when you don't know something, just say 'I don't know.'"

"Okay," he told me smiling back.

———

Thorin loved having a book read aloud to him, but reading a book with me was now intimidating. I knew he could do it but I had to figure out how to convince him he could.

"Thorin should we write a story?" I asked excitedly.

"Yeah!"

"Okay, let's come up with some characters. Who should be in it?"

"Cow! And horse!" he yelled.

"Awesome! What do they do? What's one thing they do?"

"Eat cake!"

"Big surprise." I smiled. "Okay, where's the cake?

"In kitchen. Cow and horse take it!"

"I like it! A cake caper!" I applauded.

"Should we have pictures in the story?"

"Yeah!"

Thorin had always drawn and painted. He had an easel since he was three years old and could paint for an hour at a time. He made beautiful, expressive drawings. I had never thought to exploit that passion until now.

I found the online program Art Hub for Kids, which featured videos of a father who taught his children how to draw. Thorin and I both learned how to draw a cake, a cow, and a horse that day.

———

One of the things Ward and I lamented was that Thorin never once told us what he had done at school. This went back to preschool. One of us would ask, "What did you do today? When he was younger, he would shake his head no. Later, the answer was always "don't know." We never stopped asking. In the past, we had asked for the specifics of Thorin's day when talking with the teacher or Ed Tech. We used those details to tease out a response from Thorin. It didn't matter. He never offered anything about his day.

The day we wrote our first story together, Ward asked Thorin, as he had every night for years, "What did you do today, Thorin?"

"Make story and draw!"

Ward and I looked at each. He did it!

"Thorin, that sounds great! Show me!"

Ward and I hugged each other close that night after Thorin had gone to sleep.

"He did it, Ward! He told you about his day."

"I know. Best night, ever. We're on the right track, Kari."

"I know."

———

By December, Thorin's reading went from the bag of laminated sight words from Ms. Alice to sight words in sentences to Bob Books to Dick and Jane. His math skills grew to counting to 100 and beginning addition. His learning increased more in those four months than during his entire public school education. He was half of an inch taller. And, he started taking photographs again.

I also discovered what Thorin and I were doing was a hybrid of unschooling and homeschooling. Unschooling is child directed and geared around the child's interests. Homeschooling is more curriculum based. We used curriculum for math and some language skills, and everything else I created based on Thorin's interests through daily living.

Not only did I start to see Thorin mature academically but also emotionally. Our dog Walt was fifteen years old—very old for a German shepherd—and he had serious health issues. Ward and I had talked about what would eventually happen to Walt. And, Thorin had started to notice Walt wasn't able to do the same things. The forts he built for the two of them now had a cushy bed for Walt. He told Walt it was "okay on floor" when he stopped jumping on his bed at night.

In January, Walt fell down on a walk. He wouldn't let me pick him up; instead he crawled back to the house. Once home, Thorin sat and petted Walt's head, telling him over and over, "Okay, Walty, okay." A week later, we had to put Walt to sleep.

"Where Walt now?" Thorin asked me.

"He's in heaven." To help explain, I made a rudimentary drawing complete with Walt's ascending soul.

The next day at breakfast, I saw Thorin was wearing his backpack. "What's that for?"

"For Asgard," he explained.

"You're going to Asgard?" I asked.

"Yes. To see Walty."

I realized I must have made heaven sound a lot like Thor's birthplace.

"Honey, Walt's not in Asgard."

"Yes. I go now." Thorin sounded adamant.

A few days later, Thorin had a dream about Walt.

Thorin told me, "Walt happy!"

"I know, Thorin. I know."

He started dancing around the room singing, "Walty alive at night in our dreams!"

Thorin had pulled out all the stops for his best friend, voicing a sentence that expressed all his thoughts.

⸺

I learned part of our education at home was reprogramming the previous, narrow opinions heaped on Thorin.

One day, I said to Thorin after he read a new book, "You are so smart! I'm proud of you!"

"No," he said, tears welled in his eyes.

"You are. Believe that. Okay?"

Some days, homeschooling became an exercise in how often my heart could break.

A few days later, Thorin wanted me to leave the room while he read.

"Say the words out loud though, okay?"

"Yes."

I said I was going to do the dishes but instead I tucked myself on the other side of the door to listen to him. He was doing great, then silence. When I stole a quick look, I found him staring back at me. He looked sad.

"Hey, I want this, okay?" he told me.

"Okay," I said.

I understood Thorin was as invested as I was in his learning.

Over time, I figured out at school Thorin was seen as a boy with limitations and at home I saw only his potential. Thorin's guesstimates and his trying to distract me with what he knew to be interests of mine were savvy tactics that might be used by anyone who is uncertain of himself. His long pauses that led to understanding can be applied to many of us, and not necessarily just those of us with a diagnosis. Thorin's absence of faith in himself is relatable to anyone who has ever been judged. His preferred nakedness was well within the bounds of boyhood.

At school, Thorin was perceived different from his peers in every way. Down syndrome was the single overarching principle used to understand Thorin. That restricted picture resulted in other children treating him as a baby—his most consistent complaint—and being unworthy of education by professionals. The lens I choose to understand Thorin is not distorted by his diagnosis. The lens I choose is clear and open and full of possibility.

During the month of February, my mom lived with us after she passed out in a restaurant. She was taken by ambulance to the hospital.

Thorin asked, "Bubba die?"

"No, not now," I replied trying to assure him.

My mom was more dependent on me. It was hard for both of us. Sometimes, she resented needing me, and I resented being needed. We fought about the most ridiculous things, but we also had deeper conversations. Our relationship was much richer and more honest now that it was clear it was also time-limited. She, Thorin, and I spent many days together cuddled on the couch reading. Thorin slept with her every night. Most days, I was grateful to be at home for both of them. I was supposed to be doing this.

⎯⎯

After nine months of homeschooling and spending close to ten hours per day, five days per week with Thorin, I had changed. Some changes were noticeable—I could not only cook but loved cooking. Other changes snuck up on me. I don't know exactly when it happened, but Thorin started offering daily commentary on what I was wearing.

One morning, I came into the kitchen with a head wrap on, which I thought was very chic and practical because it was humid and I have wavy hair. He looked up from his cereal grimacing.

"What's that?"

"You don't like it?"

"No, no. Off now."

"Now listen I like it . . ."

Thorin covered his eyes and said, "Very bad. No!"

I took it off.

Another day, I put on a pair of boots with my jeans tucked in.

"Oh, no. No. Go back."

"I like the way it looks!"

"Ick!" We agreed I could cuff the jeans above the ankle.

A few weeks later, a black quilted vest I ordered arrived. I put it on.

"It's great, right?" I said seeking Thorin's approval. At that point, I didn't realize I had been brainwashed.

Thorin picked up the bag it had come in and said, "Put in here now."

"I love this."

"Bad, bad, bad. No good. Ick."

I decided to ignore him. I wore it out that day. Every hour or so, he would say something, such as "really bad," "stinky, stinky," and "so sad," even signing the word "sad."

Ward hadn't actually seen the vest on me when he accompanied me to the mall store to exchange it. I shuffled through all the vests, trying each on and hating them.

"I should have brought Thorin to help me," I said aloud.

The look on Ward's face was of true concern. "What are you talking about?"

"Thorin likes to help pick out my clothes?" *Why did it sound like I was asking a question?*

Ward in very serious tone asked, "Kari, tell me exactly why you're returning the vest?"

"Thorin hates it." I realized how wacky it sounded as soon as I said it.

"Kari! Thorin is eight!" he said emphatically. In a more soothing voice, he said, "Put the vest on."

After I put it on, Ward told me, "You look great. That is a perfect cut for your body."

"It is?" I said unconvinced.

"Kari how long has this been going on?"

"I don't know . . ." I didn't want to say maybe months.

"Has it occurred to you he may have an ulterior motive in trying to manage your choices?" This sounded like an intervention.

"Oh no, he is messing with my head!" A full-on epiphany moment.

In the car ride back home, I thought about how to handle this whole situation. I realized I mustn't be direct. I didn't want him to know I had been duped. Ward helped me by making a big show of how much he loved the vest on me.

"Doesn't Mommy look beautiful?"

"Yes! Pretty Mommy!" he said beaming.

While Ward let Coco out, Thorin sidled up to me.

"Not for you! No!" He sounded like the kid in film *The Bad Seed*.

"Hey, I'm on to you!" I sounded firm in my conviction. I would be keeping the vest!

———

I was puzzled by something. Thorin still had a hard time putting sentences together when he talked, but when he read aloud, it was amazingly understandable. Ward, my mom, and Betty had also commented on the notable difference. Since homeschooling, Thorin had continued to see his out-of-school speech therapist three times a week. He had made great strides with her, but it was clear he had a way to go toward being understood. I asked her about the contrast in communication between talking and reading.

"He has apraxia."

"Apraxia?"

"It's a motor speech disorder. He knows what he wants to say, but the communication between his brain and coordinating the muscle movements necessary to say those words is blocked. Generative language is hard. When reading, he sees the words; he doesn't have to figure out what he wants to say."

"Why am I just hearing this?" I was incredulous.

"I don't know." She was blasé.

It was a lesson for me in not assuming I was getting all the information I needed about Thorin. I clearly needed to be asking more questions.

She continued, "Imagine all the thoughts he wants to express, but the opening for them to come out is a very thin straw."

I had suggested a similar hypothesis years ago—that Thorin had more to express—to his preschool speech therapist but had been discouraged by her.

"Okay," I said to his speech therapist. "This is the first time I'm hearing this from any speech therapist."

"Not all speech pathologists understand apraxia."

"So the therapy he had gotten before . . ."

She nodded her head, "Probably wasn't effective."

I imagined how much work Thorin was required to do for things most of us take for granted. Also, the phrase "thin straw" struck me; his words parsed through a straw was like his breath gasping through the same metaphor in the ER years before.

———

Each month, Thorin started a new theater class at the museum. He still didn't participate in the final performance, but it didn't detract from him enjoying the class. However, it did make me have concerns for the dance recital that was scheduled in May, particularly since we had to purchase an over-priced glitzy outfit for the end-of-the-year performance. I shared my concerns with Heather at the dance school.

"Don't worry. He'll do it. Ms. Alivia [Thorin's dance teacher] has a 100 percent success rate with recitals."

I gave her the check for his costume and hoped for the best.

The day of the dance recital arrived. And as predicted, Thorin participated in the performance in front of 200 people. He had on black slacks, a brilliant white shirt, a black vest with shiny sequins, and a pink bow tie. He'd asked to get his hair cut a few days before; it was very short and stylish. When he walked out on the stage, he looked taller than I had remembered. His head and chin were pointed up, his shoulders squared. I saw how composed he was. Thorin stopped to give a quick wave to Ward and me. Then, his focus shifted to the audience as a whole. He glowed. It was then I saw he was not doing this for us—it was for himself. For all those months, he had prepared to perform something he loved doing.

———

I was used to Thorin's Avenger inspired tales, such as "Hulk is at the library with the Baby Avengers. He eats the books and some people. The woman says 'Shhhhh!' and 'Quiet!'" But one day, he told me a violent story that I actually wanted to edit. We started the usual way.

"Okay, have you thought of characters?

It took a minute, then he said, "A Baby Robot Teacher."

"That's specific. What's the name?"

He thought for a moment more, "Um…Kicky Waters. Cries a lot."

"Kicky Waters cries a lot?"

"Yes." He had moved on from "yesith."

"Then what happens?"

"At school. Stab ten red chickens. Died."

"What?" I was horrified.

"Died. Wear glasses."

"Wait. Who's wearing glasses?" I was trying to keep up with his story.

"Chickens."

"Kicky Waters stabbed the chickens?"

"Yes! Girls and boys saw. Screamed!"

I bet they did.

"This is a horrible story."

"Yeah. Chickens zombies now."

"The chickens turned into zombies?"

"Yeah. They eat mother."

"Who ate the mother?"

"Zombie chickens."

"Could it be 'They ate humans' rather than 'They ate the mother'?" I was starting to take this personally.

"No! Not!" Thorin replied insistently.

Later, Thorin told the story to Bubba.

"Just one mother?" she asked.

"Yes, one," he said.

"Who is the mother?" she asked.

Thorin pointed at me.

"Oh, Thorin, you don't really want zombie chickens to eat your mother, do you?" she asked.

"Yes, I do."

"Thorin, if they ate your mommy who would drive you all over town?"

I wanted to think I had more to offer than transportation, but at least she was trying to keep me alive.

"Chickens," he said followed by obnoxiously accurate chewing noises.

Thorin went off to play.

"He's imaginative," my mom said.

"I hope that's what it is."

I put out a Facebook post asking for parental feedback. The best answer was from a friend who taught literature and was also a mother: "Stories and imagination are the places they get to transgress with impunity. Let him go!" So I did. I wrote up the story, and we used it as part of his reading. To go with his story, Thorin drew a robot, a zombie chicken, and me.

———

As our first year of unschooling came to end, I took Thorin to his favorite Mexican restaurant for our end-of-the-school-year celebration lunch. He and I hadn't talked much about his last year of public school, but it seemed like a good opportunity to open the door.

"Thorin, do you miss going to school?"

"I miss Walt," told me mournfully.

"I know, me too. But, not school?"

"Not school," he said.

"I've been wracking my brains trying to think of your first grade teacher's name." I had developed a block when it came to her.

Thorin kept his head down eating.

"Thorin, I can see her plain as day, what's her name?"

"Kicky Waters," he said.

My heart sank. "Oh, no! Really?"

"Yes."

While I was taking in what he said, I remembered her name.

"Mrs. Bruce! She's Baby Robot Teacher, Kicky Waters?"

"Yes!" he said unequivocally.

"Can I ask one more question?"

"Yes! Yes!"

"Last year, I asked if you knew what the problem was at school. You said, 'I do. It's me.'"

Thorin nodded his head.

"Do you still think that's true?" I asked.

"No." His voice was strong. I believed him.

"You know it's them?"

"Yes," he said smiling.

"We should have left school earlier." Remorse filled my voice.

"Yes."

"Daddy and I are so sorry, you know that, right?" I felt horrible.

"It's okay," he said.

"No, it's not. Thorin, what did you think about in school? How did you do it, Thorin?"

"King of Asgard."

"The King of Asgard?"

"Odin's son, King of Asgard."

"You were Thor? That's how you did it?"

"Yes."

"Oh, Thorin, brilliant!" I willed myself to hold back tears. Thorin was not upset. This moment was not about me but about him.

He smiled.

We continued silently enjoying our food. I felt a wave inside me take me back to the previous year, creating the Pictello presentation for class: Thorin insisting on dressing as Thor and then looking into the camera to say, "I am Thor." Sitting in the restaurant with Thorin, I placed my hands on the table to ground myself, the same as I did the day I met him. Thorin had told his classmates, whether they understood or not, that he was powerful. My son is powerful; the thumping in my heart made it true.

I fell further into past memories to the day I told Thorin he had Down syndrome. I had feared for him. I wanted to protect him. I knew him well enough to know I must tell him he had super powers like the Avengers he loved. Together they are invincible, just like our family.

I'm back to the present again. I have stopped eating. I look at Thorin, his size belittling the multitudes he contains. Whitman is whispering.

I fall back to the day Ward suggested the blog be called Thunder Boy, based on Thorin's name. We never considered the Avengers. Prescient?

Finally, as the wave brought me back, I thought of Thorin's parents who had named him after Thorin Oakenshield, the leader of the Company of Dwarves in *The Hobbit*, who makes the heroic journey to reclaim the Lonely Mountain from the fearsome dragon Smaug. Sitting across from Thorin, it was easy for me to imagine him as a hero who survived the challenges placed upon him. I prayed deeply that the legacy of his namesake portended a life of adventure, accomplishments, and love even I couldn't imagine for him.

Updates on the unusual journey
of Thorin, Kari, and Ward
can be found at

ATYPICALSON.COM